EASTER AND SPRINGTIME
Six Playscripts about New Life

EASTER HOPE, LIFE IS TOO SHORT FOR WAR –
An anti-war pageant set in a framework of
traditional melodies.

THE GOOD SHEPHERD –
SOLDIERS FOR THE DAWN –
THE OLD TRAMP AND EASTER –
The symbolism of the springtime is presented
in three Easter plays.

THE EASTER CAT –
The tragedy of a loved one's sudden death
contrasts with the arrival of an Easter kitten.

ZAKOTU THE WEREWOLF –
It is Eastertime and mysterious murders have been
taking place in the remote villages of the great
swamplands.

Playscripts are all suitable for production or reading
aloud and the music is in tonic sol-fa.

LIFE OF DREW CARSON

Sam Drew Carson was born in the North of Ireland and educated there at Wellington College and the Ulster Polytechnic. He completed his education in the USA at New Mexico Highlands University and the University of Arkansas and has traveled widely in North America, around the Atlantic and in Europe.

Drew worked as a seaman and fish-gutter in Vestmannaeyjar off the coast of Iceland. He lived and worked in the Irish and Western Isles Gaeltachts and was married in Welsh-speaking Carmarthen after which he honeymooned in Belfast. He has told his stories, composed and sung his songs, seeking storylines in Bristol and the English Westcountry. Drew has also lived and written in Nashville, Tennessee, in the wooded hills of Mid-America and from the Appalachians to the Ozarks. This was the culture that gave rise to the now worldwide Scotch-Irish country music.

In the USA, he also worked beside the bayous of the French-speaking Cajuns in the South and among the Western Spanish-speaking Navajos, Apaches and Pueblos of the Sangre de Cristo Mountains in New Mexico.

Drew has sailed far into the seas of old Gaelic and Oriental legend. After many years searching for inspiration for story and music, the author is still traveling and writing.

BOOKS BY THE SAME AUTHOR

SEE YOU AROUND
Pantomime of Bygone Fun and Frolic
ISBN: 978-1-908184-08-5
CULT OF THE WIDOW VIDOVA
Detective Felix O'Neill in a Crime Adventure
ISBN: 978-1-908184-09-2
WHITE ZOMBIES OF NEW CASTILE
A Sci-Fi Adventure
ISBN: 978-1-908184-10-8
EASTER AND SPRINGTIME
Six Playscripts about New Life
ISBN: 978-1-908184-12-2

Easter and Springtime

Six Playscripts about New Life

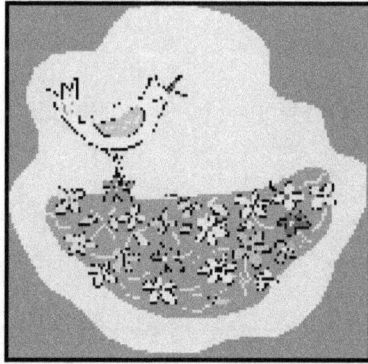

DREW CARSON

Legals

Published by S. A. Carson,
29 Northleaze, Long Ashton, Bristol BS41 9HS, UK
Publisher's email: verygoodreading@googlemail.com

PLAYSCRIPTS:
Life is Too Short for War, The Good Shepherd, Soldiers for the Dawn, The Old Tramp and Easter, The Easter Cat, Zakotu the Werewolf

ISBN: 978-1-908184-12-2

CONTENTS

Page

Easter Hope - Life is Too Short for War

ABOUT THE PLAY

A soldier went to war. He looked well and strong.

Out in a foreign field a wedding took place but it was bombed from the sky. Men and women and children died.

As time passed, the soldier could hardly be recognized by his friends for he had been wounded badly, as had others.

The wounded soldier now tottered along in the reflection of the flares in the red sky. Now the handsome young soldier's appearance was changing. All the soldiers limped along to the beat of the battle drums. Then the soldiers began to stumble and fall as they were killed or became wounded and weak. One by one the stretchers and coffins took them away as the sounds of battle formed a dark choir around them.

At home the pot plants became dried up and drooped.

Their friends and comrades asked, "Where are the storms and rains that used to come and go so suddenly? Where are the keen young soldiers now? Laid low. Where indeed are the nurses and friends, the sweethearts, the children, the wives of times past?"

They had become the dead of war. Or they had all gone to the gravesides to hear the echoes of mourning.

As for the soldiers, the war had begun with a strong stride out. It continued with a red fire glowing in the sky, then a loud noise and a sharp wound, a stumbling fall, a staggering, a collapse and at the end a silent drizzle of tears.

The lifetime of the young person that should have taken eighty years to complete, with laughter and plans and fulfillment and friends and fun, had been compressed into a few short twisted months of turmoil and pain.

Then the sights and sounds of a new wedding give renewed hope for a life that will be free from war.

THE PLAYSCRIPT
OUTLINE OF THE PLAY
SCENE ONE: The Wedding
SCENE TWO: The Singer of Freedom
SCENE THREE: The Guns of Greed
SCENE FOUR: Another Wedding
PRODUCTION NOTES
Place: A country house - full stage - overlooking a garden - downstage.

Time Period: The play can be set anywhere in time of war with uniforms appropriate to any period. Some possible choices are: Napoleonic Wars - early 18th Century, late 19th Century, e.g., Indian, South African, Crimean, WW1 (1914-1918), WW2 (1939-1945), Indo-China Wars - mid 20th Century, e.g., Vietnam, Korea.

The wartime period chosen will always depend

on the history of the country of production. Asian, Russian, South American, African, Indian, Mid-Eastern are all recommended as alternatives to Western Culture.

<u>Stage Time:</u>

45-60 minutes with one or two short breaks

<u>Age Groups</u>

Over 13, teens and adults

<u>Music</u>

Background music and songs. Five songs with simple, catchy traditional tunes for good voices, trained or untrained: *Johnny I Hardly Knew You, The Wedding, The Singer of Freedom, Guns of Greed, Sweethearts Lost in War.*

Background piano, drums, reed (whistle, pipes, fife or other military). Basic musical notation is given in tonic sol-fa.

<u>Set</u>

One, with two backdrops.

<u>Handicap Suitability</u>

Teens and Upwards

Suitable for visually handicapped –

music and song.

Suitable for vocally handicapped –

mime and tableaux.

      The uniforms of the soldiers, the furniture, the dresses of the ladies, the soldiers' swords and accoutrements, whether carried or as part of the props and décor - all of these should be of the same time period - to be chosen by the producer/director. The key concept here is *consistency* in décor and dress. The background music and song has been adapted so as to be universal in its appeal.

All the acting is in mime. None of the actors speak at any time during the entire production. The songs may be given as a live presentation on or near the stage or played on tape or disc in the background. The term 'stage' throughout always means 'acting area' whether raised up or on the same level as cameras and audience.

CHARACTERS IN THE PLAY

In total, about six male and seven female actors will be needed plus more soldiers may be used as extras if the stage production is large or elaborate but no more than four or five ladies as mothers, sisters or wives, should be present at any one time.

Musicians (three or more): A chorus and military band group - voice, pipes, piano, reed (e.g., tin whistle, fife, recorder, flute). These musicians may be on or offstage and are to sing and play the six songs as background to the mime. If onstage, they should be in a peripheral position, e.g., grouped to left or rightstage or lined up along each side of the stage. If offstage, they may be in the pit or to right or left offstage.

Minister of Religion;

Two Bridesmaids;

Two Child Attendants - optional.

SCENE ONE
THE WEDDING

Scene: *The drawing room and garden of a large country house.*

Up and middle-stage is an open-view of the drawing room, its walls lined with military paintings, young and fresh green pot-plants, swords, portraits of soldiers and their ladies, medals, plaques and trophies of war.

In the leftstage far corner is a piano with its back diagonally towards the audience and a piano stool in the corner behind the piano.

Centerstage is a space for dancing. To the right, along the wall, are easy chairs and sofas, coffee tables and ottomans. Left and upstage is a dining table and chairs. Mid-stage, the back wall of the drawing room is taken up largely with French windows which are open and leading into a garden. The floor may be polished wood effect with scatter rugs or may be carpeted.

Downstage beside the French windows are curtains on each side, now open, but closed in later scenes, opening out into a garden and pathway with a broad walkway of concrete or pebbles or gravel stretching from left to right-stage. On the nearside are tall flowers and on the far side of the pathway there is a backdrop with hedges, sky and trees and a large fountain.   There are a few deckchairs or picnic tables and chairs scattered around.   The French windows are very broad and act like curtains to a stage beyond the stage.

Enter: From right into the garden, four or five soldiers who meet and greet and toast, much raising of hats and bowing.

Enter: From left into the garden four or five ladies who join the meeting and greeting.

Enter: A young soldier and his wife, from right into the main room, hand in hand.   His uniform and her dress are appropriate to the chosen time period. A background tune is playing. This scene is one of happy marriage, youth and hope. The young soldier and his wife dance across the floor. Downstage in the outside *garden the group of soldiers still slap and joke with each other. They are joined, through the French windows, by the young soldier and his dancing lady.*

Enter: *A pianist, male or female, who sits behind the piano.*

Female Voice Sings:
JOHNNY I HARDLY KNEW YOU
Sung: Steady and Warlike

VERSE ONE:

     t_1 - t_1 m   m   m   fe   s   fė   s
With your guns and drums and drums and guns
m - *r* t_1 - *r*
Haroo, Haroo
    t_1 - t_1 m   m   m   fe   s   fe   s
With your drums and guns and guns and drums
   l - *t*   s - *t*
Haroo, Haroo
     s - s   t   t   t   s   l   l   l
With your guns and drums and drums and guns
  s   s - s   s   s   m - fe   fe
All the nice girls will pursue you
  s   l   t   s   l
O the truth to tell
  fe   s   m   fe
You look so well
  m   m - m   m   m - r   m   *m*
O   Johnny I   hardly knew you

With your guns and drums and drums and guns
Haroo, Haroo
With your drums and guns and guns and drums
Haroo, Haroo
With your guns and drums and drums and guns
All the nice girls will pursue you
O the truth to tell
You look so well
O Johnny I hardly knew you

In the background, in the garden there are happy scenes in this downstage area. Vapors and mists may float around these visions of young soldiers preparing to go to war, in cheer and hope and self-confidence. The ladies may be younger as sisters or wives or somewhat older as mothers.

Outside the downstage French windows, near the driveway at picnic tables, surrounded by flowers, bushes and trees, the group of some five or six uniformed soldiers and their ladies continue relaxing and sharing glasses and snacks. They are casual and sober. They bow and shake hands with each other in a polite semi-formal and cheerful way.

Enter: From left, into the drawing room, comes the bridegroom - a soldier in full dress followed by his fellow soldiers and their ladies.

Enter: From right, the pianist, a lady who sits at the piano.

Enter: From left, a beautiful and formally-dressed bride who walks among the soldiers. They toast her pleasantly and respectfully.

Enter: From left, a minister of religion, two bridesmaids and a best man. Child attendants are optional.

One of the soldiers acts as the best-man, one as father of the bride. The scene becomes one of a happy wedding lit up by youth and hope.

The bride and groom stand center-stage to cheers and throwing of rice and confetti. The scene may be varied to suit any religion or secular marriage.

Some of the guests, here assembled, now enter the garden downstage. The scene ends with a tableau of everyone bowing and toasting towards the young lady and her husband, who stand by the fountain in the garden.

Life is Too Short for War

Throughout the Scene a

Female Voice Sings:

THE WEDDING
(based on an actual incident)
Sung: Slowly and Sadly

VERSE ONE:

s_1 - l_1 t_1 l_1 t_1 r_1 r_1 - r_1 t_1 - l_1 - s_1
The bride and the groom stood hand in hand

r_1 m_1 s_1 - s_1 - s_1 l_1 s_1
A bright and devoted pair

t_1 - d   r   r - r   r t_1 r - m   m - r
They wed and they danced in a brief dreamland

t_1 - l_1 s_1 m_1 d t_1 l_1
And they saw their future there

t_1 - d   r - r   r t_1 r   m m   r
But the guns of doom in a deadly band

t_1 s_1 m_1 d t_1 l_1
Were threatening in the air

s_1 l_1 t_1 l_1 - t_1 - r_1 r_1 - r_1 t_1 l_1 s_1
And the theatre of war went high and grand

r_1 - r_1 m_1 - s_1 s_1 l_1 s_1
In the drama of despair

VERSE ONE:
The bride and the groom stood hand in hand
A bright and devoted pair
They wed and they danced in a brief dreamland
And they saw their future there
But the guns of doom in a deadly band
Were threatening in the air
And the theatre of war went high and grand
In the drama of despair

VERSE TWO:
For death fell down from the sky that day
As guns shot out their darts
They calmly killed in a dread display
Of the murdermaster's arts.
Like broken dolls small children lay
All tossed around in parts
As the guns blew the bride and groom away
And the futures of our hearts

Enter: The soldiers from right to downstage garden, marching to the roll and rattle of drums.

The soldiers form up in line, including the former groom and best-man, swords drawn. They march forward, just a few paces, in slow step, then pause in tableau. Swords are still raised as the next song is sung with piano, fife, drum or pipe accompanying the female voice.

All remain in Tableau as a tableau of soldiers as before is revealed lined up in the garden.

Enter: *Ladies from left into down-stage garden holding handkerchiefs.*

Female Voice Sings as the ladies bid farewell to the soldiers. The ladies line up courteously in front of the soldiers. The ladies face the audience then wave goodbye with their handkerchiefs as the soldiers march off stage left. The music becomes fierce and proud.

The female voice is accompanied by martial instrumentals such as a strict drumbeat, fife or bagpipes, as she sings **The Wedding.**

As the drums beat intensively, the soldiers salute the ladies who are still downstage from the soldiers and still facing the audience. As the soldiers march offstage to the left, the music ceases suddenly. The ladies, looking after them, handkerchiefs in air, remain in tableau as

<u>Curtain</u>

SCENE TWO
THE SINGER OF FREEDOM

Scene: *The same country house interior.*

The French windows are closed and leaves are seen blowing around outside.

A soldier is discovered sitting right on one of the couches in the drawing room. His right arm is in a sling and his face is masked.

Enter: *His lady weeping gently, distressed, dabbing her eyes with a white handkerchief. She kneels slowly at some two or three feet before the soldier and stretches out to take his hand.*

Tableau

During the singing of the next background song, this tableau is varied only slightly by the soldier raising or lowering his head and the lady ceasing to use and lowering the handkerchief, then finally raising her head, no longer weeping. At the end of the scene, the lady stands and bows, finally smiling sadly and remotely. The soldier sits upright, bravely but shattered.

During this scene the background song, preferably with some piano support: French windows still shut, with leaves outside.

Enter: The same lady as in Scene One. Now there is a more somber, cool and sinister atmosphere. There is an implied doubt - to fight or not to fight? Is it all worth it? The soldier of the previous scene does not appear. His lady enters the same room alone, walks around viewing plants that are now withering. She is weeping and disconsolate. She sits at the piano facing the audience. She plays or appears to play the piano in a slow march with other instruments backing the singer. She looks sadly into the distance as she plays.

Female Voice Sings:
THE SINGER OF FREEDOM

THE SINGER OF FREEDOM
Sung: Warlike and Steady

VERSE ONE:

s_1 d - d   r   f - m   r   d   m   s d^1
The singer of freedom sows the truthful seeds
t d^1 l   s   s   m - f   s   m   r   d
In meadows where streams of truth are flowing
s_1 d   d   r   f - m   r   d   m   s d^1
The sharp sword of honor cuts away the weeds
t d^1 l   s   s   m   f   s   m   r   d
As brambles of hate and fear are growing

The singer of freedom sows the truthful seeds
In meadows where streams of truth are flowing
The sharp sword of honor cuts away the weeds
As brambles of hate and fear are growing

The scene is dimly lit except that the spotlight or lighting system searches out the same garden beyond the French windows which are now open. This scene represents a time of somber doubt, self-searching and some wounding, though not yet absolute disaster or remorse.

Enter: *From left, into the garden the same soldiers as in Scene One. The lone soldier from left. He walks slowly, a broken figure, leaning on a cane. He approaches and puts his arms around the* *sobbing lady and begins to lead her gently towards offstage right.*

The lights span the entire set, emphasizing that the soldier's lady is on her own at the piano. She remains still in tableau as the lights fade.

The tempo is slowed down and a female voice sings to stately, deliberate, even sinister music. The music - fife, drum, piano, pipes or other - reflects a wounded time of life. The drums are a rattle of fear and tremble uncertainly at times. Things are beginning to fall apart and the self-confidence of Act One is now entirely gone. **Female Voice Sings:**

With your guns and drums and drums and guns.
Haroo, Haroo
With your drums and guns and guns and drums.
Haroo, Haroo
With your guns and drums and drums and guns
All our kind care will renew you
But my limping lad
You look so bad
O Johnny I hardly knew you
O my darling boy
They stole your joy
And Johnny I hardly knew you

As the song ends, the last wounded soldier is led towards stage right exit by his mother, wife or sister. The lights dim to the level where the two figures are seen about to LEAVE stage <u>only</u> in silhouette.

Lights dim even more and fade out. The two figures, about to leave are still right-stage and downstage and freeze in tableau.

<u>Curtain</u>

SCENE THREE
THE GUNS OF GREED

Scene: *The same. The pot-plants are drooping, withered, wintry and dried, as though they had been neglected and were lacking in water. The lights in the drawing room are dim. The lone lady from the last scene, now somewhat older, perhaps 60 plus, enters stage left and looks around sadly. As the background song is sung and played slowly with piano and pipes lamenting, she makes a tour of the room, looking in turn at all the withered flowers and plants, some on the floor. The French windows are closed* *once again and leaves can be seen scattering outside.*

With your guns and drums and drums and guns,
Haroo, Haroo
With your drums and guns and guns and drums,
Haroo, Haroo
With your drums and guns and guns and drums
The birds of the battle slew you
O they swooped down low
And they screamed hello
Oh Johnny I hardly knew you

Towards the end of the song, the lady sits behind the piano and plays along with the last few notes. As the song ends she rises.

Lady Leaves *stage right as lights emphasize the leaves and fallen flowers:*

The drawing room is as before, dimly lit and the light focuses on the downstage outdoor garden area where the French windows are now open.

The outdoor garden scene has now been modified by a backdrop which represents a battle scene of flares and firework. If the previous backdrop was neutral, for example clouds and hills, it may be quite feasible to achieve a battlefield effect by way of shadows and lighting only, without a new backdrop. Lighting should throw shadows on the path and flowered foreground and create circles of light in the sky.

*   **Enter:**   The previous wounded soldiers to the garden area from left to right.*

*   For the rest of this scene an occasional gun booms or rattles as the now mature soldiers bowed and limping and slow of step trudge across the garden area with guns on their shoulders and in their arms.   This parade turns and wearily retraces its steps until end of scene.   The battlefield lights up behind them as a male voice sings to the accompaniment of drums, piano, pipes, reed.*

*   Male Voice Sings:*

THE GUNS OF GREED

> s d^{1}t t l l   t d^1 t-l   s
> O Singer of freedom, Tell of daring deeds
>   s   l   m - m   s l t d^l
> Bold springs that flow forever
>   s$_1$ d   d r f m r   d   m   s   d^1
> Let drums of the liar and the guns of greed
> t - d^1 l - s s   m   f   s - m   r d
> Be drowned in that true and fearless river.

O Singer of freedom, Tell of daring deeds
Bold springs that flow forever
Let drums of the liar and the guns of greed
Be drowned in that true and fearless river.

A last salvo of guns is heard, the soldiers walk with weary shoulders across the downstage area which is now a field of battle. This area is now lit up by flares (e.g., red paint and flashing lights or fireworks). As the background song ends, they stand still in a tableau representing bitter warfare and the drudgery of military logistics.

The French windows are still open. Both the indoor drawing room and the outdoor garden and battlefield are empty.

The downstage area is now lit to show some of the vegetation of the garden as props but the backdrop battlefield effect remains.

The guns are now silent and the flares no longer flash. The drawing room, mid and upstage, is well enough lit to make clear the faded flowers and drooping plants but the room is not fully lit up, perhaps in a medium blue light with some red or yellow highlights. A long bristled broom and a rose should be at hand just to the side of the French windows.

Enter: *From stage-right any one of the now mature ladies. She walks sadly around the room and pauses at the French windows, leaning against the wall and looking across at the downstage garden. She presents at first a straight profile to the audience. However, she turns painfully towards the audience, upstage, from time to time, as the background song is sung with only a light piano or plaintive pipe accompaniment.*

The lady takes up a rose and scatters the petals and leaves over the garden. Then she takes up the broom and begins to sweep out into the garden all the leaves and flowers around the drawing room.

As the leaves are swept out of the French windows, she pauses once again presenting a profile, with tearful head bowed low, to the audience. She remains in tableau.

The tone of this sub-scene, in sharp contrast to the previous scene, is fairly loud, intense and reflects the bitter, cruel and grim reality of war rather than its pathos, passion, or soul-stirring. The final few moments however revert to a very brief quiet time of pity and regret for the fallen.

Rattling marching drums, martial pipes, brisk piano, sharp reed, as available, are any and all acceptable as background instrumental. The female voice that sings the words is likewise plaintive, intense, resentful and above all afflicted, suffering and heartrending.

The interior of the drawing room is much the same as in the last scene except *that the lighting is slightly more dimmed. The focus of the lighting is on the downstage garden beyond the still open French windows. The garden is now symbolically a battle and burial scene.*

The farthest perimeter of downstage backcloth is now covered with tombstones from one side to the other, whether as the usual rounded rectangles or as crosses or as coffin-shaped wooden monuments, depending on the cultural perceptions of the audience. The details here are to be chosen by the director.

The backdrop (or lights) behind this graveyard is as before, a battlefield lit up by flares, circles and flashes of light or candles as symbols of death. This area of symbolic death is lit just well enough for the audience to recognize a reminiscent parade of ALL the previous soldiers now long dead in battle.

__Enter__ left and __exit__ right the parade of dead soldiers.

They are followed by their ladies (mothers, sisters or wives) also walking across the scene from left-stage to exit right-stage. The parading soldiers should be downcast, sad, crushed and tired. In contrast they are followed by their ladies, upright, straight, with heads in air but weeping as they face the skies. The ladies also enter left and some exit right, while some later remain on stage in tableau.

The faint sound of guns and explosions fill the air on ONLY a few (three or four) occasions. The symbolic procession of dead soldiers followed by their living ladies will slowly become seen as black silhouettes surrounded by wisps of smoke, if the sharpness of the lighting permits. In the absence of really good lighting, including a good viewing angle from the audience, the scene may be, well lit at first, and may become simply a dimly lit, misty, smoky procession of soldiers and ladies.

Female Voice Sings *as the procession takes place.*

With your guns and drums and drums and guns
Haroo, Haroo
With your drums and guns and guns and drums
Haroo, Haroo
With your drums and guns and guns and drums
It made me weep to view you
For I saw you sleep
And you slept so deep
O Johnny I hardly knew you

Male and Female Voices now Sing
(slowly and with deep feeling)

SWEETHEARTS LOST IN WAR
Sung: Slow and Stately

VERSE ONE:

l - fe r m fe s   m l s m - r   r   de   r
O where are the rains that fell on winters past and gone?

l l r^1 t   r^1 de^1 l   t   s   m   m
Where are the storms that wrecked good ships from

fe   s   l
dusk to dawn?

l l r^1 t - r^1 de^1 l   t   s   m - m   fe   s   l
Where are the hails and sleets that froze down from the
sky?

s - m - r   m fe   s - m   l s   m   r   r r
Ah, where are the sweethearts of the good times gone by?

VERSE ONE:
O where are the rains that fell
on winters past and gone?
Where are the storms that wrecked
good ships from dusk to dawn?
Where are the hails and sleets
that froze down from the sky?
Ah, where are the sweethearts
of the good times gone by?

VERSE TWO:
Where are the battle drums
that led so fierce and proud?
Where are the raging guns
that fired so red and loud?
Where are the dread young men
who marched to fight and die?
Ah, where are the sweethearts
of the good times gone by?

Tableau:

Towards the end of the song, the last two or three of the ladies, walking past the graves, stand still and remain with bowed heads in a weeping posture, in tableau, as snow begins to fall on the tombs. The snow trickles straight down but flurries thrown in and blown in from left and right may also be added.

SCENE FOUR
ANOTHER WEDDING

The scene changes with buds appearing on the trees as spring approaches. The birds sing again and the first daffodils and crocuses appear. The sound of another wedding party can be heard in the distance as church bells ring out. Laughter and singing is heard once more as the cycle of life continues.

The guests at the new wedding are heard to sing (on or offstage) the first four lines of verse one of **The Wedding** *from Scene One.*

> The bride and the groom stood hand in hand
> A bright and devoted pair
> They wed and they danced in a brief dreamland
> And they saw their future there

Curtain
END OF PLAYSCRIPT

The Good Shepherd

About the Play

The event took place at a hill known as the Skull. It was dark. Three persons were clearly discernible on three crosses. The shadows of kneeling, bowed figures were at the foot of the crosses. A slight murmur of grief was heard in the background.

Nearby was a garden with bushes, trees and flowers. The sky and garden remained mostly in darkness and only the shadowy outline of the crucifixion was seen. On raised ground nearby, a great stone blocked the entrance to a large cave in which the body of Jesus had been placed.

An angel appeared at the grave. It had a fierce face, colored with streaks of fire like lightning. Its robes were white as snow. It rolled back the stone from the grave revealing an empty cave with only a shroud and separately a headband, both lying on a stone slab. The angel entered the tomb with a gesture of triumph and sat on the stone slab.

The angel spoke to the friends of Jesus outside the tomb. "He is not here, he is arisen. Why seek the living among the dead. Remember what Jesus said to you in Galilee that he, the Son of Man, would be betrayed and given into the hands of wickedness and crucified by hanging upon a tree. But that, on the third day after he was hanged, he would rise up.

"Jesus said, I am the bread of life - he that cometh to me shall never hunger. Therefore, go you into all the world and publish this good news to every living creature."

The angel told them that this was a new beginning; a new springtime for the world.

The Playscript

AN EASTER PAGEANT IN ONE ACT WITH SONGS

OUTLINE OF THE PLAY

SCENE ONE: The Shadow of the Cross
SCENE TWO: The Watchers
SCENE THREE: The Good Shepherd

PRODUCTION NOTES

One Set in Three Scenes, Six Actors, a Choir.

Actors: Three Male, Four male or Four Male, Three Female.

(Angel may be either Male or Female)

The voice of a narrator - live or recorded.

Stage Time: 45-80 minutes.

Age Groups: All.

Nine Songs: *The Good Shepherd, Watchmen in the Night, Praise to Jesus, Let God be Kind, Jesus You are Living, My Humble Heart, The Living Door, The Risen One, The Good Lord is our Shepherd.*

The straightforward Biblical story of the death and resurrection of Jesus Christ is presented with songs and Choir. All verses may be sung to traditional church music or recited without music.

CHARACTERS IN THE PLAY
The Angel of the Tomb (male or female),
Mary Magdalene,
Mary the Mother,
Salome the Disciple,
Simon Peter the Disciple,
John the Disciple,
The Choir of Angels,
A Narrator,
Silhouettes of Jesus
(slides, film or painted props)

SCENE ONE
THE SHADOW OF THE CROSS

TIME: Night. The crucifixion is seen in silhouette shadow, full life size, top to bottom of far left-stage and rising high over the rest of the set, forming the left "wall" or sidedrop of the set. Three persons are clearly discernible on three crosses and the shadows of kneeling, bowed figures are at the feet of the three crosses. A slight murmur of grief is heard, lowly in the background. This crucifixion scene only is in silhouette.

The rest of the set, which is in darkness, is a garden with bushes, trees, flowers and a narrow path running the full length of front-stage then winding and rising up to a bushy knoll at top right-stage. At top of the knoll there are high bushes. The backdrop is a sky with the morning sun shining in rays of red and orange.

Throughout Scene One the sky and garden remain in darkness and only the shadowy outline of the crucifixion is lit, left-stage. Right-stage, on raised ground, is a large stone cave - a great stone stands in front of the cave entrance. This stone may be on concealed wheels for ease of opening later.

NARRATOR:

In the beginning God created the Heavens
And the Earth
And in the later times God's Son
Jesus of Nazareth went about the country
Preaching the good news
That God's Kingdom was coming
To the earth
That God was going to heal the people
Of all their sickness
And Jesus healed the sick
And raised up the dead
As proof that he was sent
By God the Creator
And he told the people
To turn away from their wickedness
And selfishness and thieving and murders
And he called upon the people to trust God
To meet their needs in this life
And in the next life
And he told them
Not to trust in their own grasping and greed

Jesus taught the people
That the whole earth from man to sparrow
Is all part of the great creation of God
And that God would look after everyone
The sparrow, the tree, the lilies of the field
The animals the rivers
The earth and all the people
If only they would stop being so selfish
And if only they would love
And respect each other
If only people would show kindness
And generosity to each other
And not go to war
Or murder each other

And the people loved Jesus and followed him
But the leaders of religion were envious
Of his power and his popularity
And they had him arrested
On the false charge
That he was speaking against God
And they bribed false witnesses
To give lying testimony against him in court
So they framed him
And demanded that the Governor
Should hang him
Now the Governor knew

That Jesus was innocent
But alas this Governor was a weak man
And did not stand by his belief
Or his word
And the crafty religious leaders
Threatened the Governor
That they would lead a revolt
Against the Governor
And destroy the city
And see to it that many would die
If the Governor did not hang Jesus

So the weak Governor
Allowed Jesus to be hanged
With two ordinary criminals
One on each side of him
The three were nailed to pieces of wood
And left to hang there until they died
And Jesus trusted his soul to God
And the soul left his body like a bird flying
And Jesus died. It was a bad death for Jesus
And also for the others
In fact, the death of Jesus
Was so terrible and terrifying
That God and his whole creation
Cried out in sympathy with Jesus
For the earth shook and mighty cliffs

The Good Shepherd

And mountains split open
And graves opened and rejected
Their visitors with dismay
As the dead bodies of holy men woke up
And walked about
And the whole land was in darkness
For three hours
Even though it was daytime
It is a terrible thing to kill
A good man

And the friends of Jesus
Took down the body of Jesus from the tree
And they bathed the body in spices
A heavy mixture of myrrh and aloes
To take away some of the smell of death
Then they wrapped the body in linen clothes
And they buried it
Inside a tomb carved out of a solid rock
In a nearby garden
Now this tomb belonged
To a rich man who was a follower of Jesus
This carved-out cave of solid rock had no
Way to get in or out except by the front door
And the front door was closed
With a massive rock

Now Jesus, when he was teaching the people
Had said - "On the third day after my death
I will rise again."

So the leaders of religion
Went to the Governor and said
"Governor, this man was a deceiver,
A confidence trickster and a liar and fraud
Who claimed that he would waken up
From death three days after he died
His followers are also frauds and liars
And cheats and they may well come
And steal the body of Jesus and hide it away
So they will pretend that Jesus
Arose from the dead
And walked away
Governor put a guard on the tomb
For at least three days
So that this confidence trick will not
Be perpetrated on the public
That way Jesus will be proven to be a fraud."
So the Governor said, "Do this yourselves.
Put your own watchmen to stand guard
Over the tomb."

So the religious leaders who had had
Jesus killed
Made sure that his body could not be stolen

They blocked up the tomb and made sure
That the huge stone that closed over the tomb
Was solid and strong and sealed
Then they sent guards - experienced soldiers
To watch over the tomb day and night
Until the three days would be over

For Jesus had said
That after three days he would arise
From the dead
As a sign for his followers
That one day they too would arise
From the dead
When God comes to call up his loved ones
Into eternal life
So it was that the watchmen in the night
Continued to guard the tomb before sunrise
Right up to the third night after the death
And burial of Jesus

*The entire front-stage is lighted enough
to see the Choir.*

Enter the Choir of Angels *who
form neat rows or circles, front-stage
center or right, look at the shadow of the
crosses, left, and at times point to them, in
unison, as they speak or sing. While
speaking or singing the Choir occasionally*

should regroup, reform or kneel to give some life and enthusiasm and slight movement to the scene.

They sing:
THE GOOD SHEPHERD
(Tune: The 23rd Psalm)

> **VERSE ONE:**
>
> d   l   taw   s d^1 taw   s   f   m   f
>
> The Lord is   my shepherd - He meets my needs
>
> l   l   s   s   t   t d^1
>
> He gives me green fields to rest
>
> l   l   taw   l   s   l   taw d^1 taw   l
>
> He leads me   beside the waters of peace
>
> l   s   taw r^1 f   m   f
>
> My soul is made whole and blessed

VERSE ONE:
The Lord is my shepherd He meets my needs
He gives me green fields to rest
He leads me beside the waters of peace
My soul is made whole and blessed

VERSE TWO:
With Him I do good for his name is Good
When valleys are dark and drear
And I must walk through the shadow of death
I never will walk with fear

VERSE THREE:
For you walk beside me in all of my ways
Your guidance and strength are here
You lay out a meal of blessings for me
That all who have doubts may see

VERSE FOUR:
You pour out the oil of good life on me
You pour it out more and more
Your goodness and mercy dwell with me now
And will do for evermore

All leave the stage

Curtain

SCENE TWO
THE WATCHERS

Time: Dawn. *Scene:* The Same, i.e. the Garden of the Tomb, center-stage and right now lit.

Enter Mary the Mother, Mary Magdalene and Salome. They wear Eastern robes and headdress. They carry baskets and herbs.

Enter Choir: (speaking or singing)

WATCHMEN IN THE NIGHT
(Tune: O For a Thousand Tongues or Lyngham)

VERSE ONE:

d   m   f   s-l-s-f-m   f m   d   r   t₁ *d*

O bless the Lord of Life all you who serve so well

m   f m   r   d   r

As watchmen in the night

r   m-r-m f   s l   s fe *s*

As witnesses and watchmen in the night

s s   s m r d m f m r d   r

Searching for truth in what you hear and see and know

s₁ d r   m

Until the morn

d f f   f f   *m*

Until the morning light

m r   r r-m-f-r s

Until the morning light

s l   s   f m   r r   *d*

Until the truthful morning light

VERSE ONE:

O bless the Lord of Life all you who serve so well
As watchmen in the night
As witnesses and watchmen in the night
Searching for truth in what you hear and see and know
Until the morn
Until the morning light
Until the morning light
Until the truthful morning light

VERSE TWO:
O bless the Lord of Life all you who serve so well
As watchmen for the day
As witnesses and watchmen for the day
Guarding the poor and weak from robbers and from wrong
Lift up your hands
Lift up your hands to pray
Lift up your hands to pray
Lift up your faithful hands to pray

VERSE THREE:
And may the Lord of Life who made the earth and skies
Who set the heavens above
Who scattered all the stars in heaven up above
Help the true watchman live for faithfulness and truth
And bless you now
And bless you now with love
And bless you now with love
And bless the watchman now with love

Choir leaves stage left.

MARY THE MOTHER:
(concerned and worried)
The stone against the cave is big and heavy.
Now, who will help us, who is strong enough?
Whom can we get to roll the stone away?

Mary Magdalene shakes her head. Salome shrugs and spreads her hands. They are worried. Suddenly there is a flash of lightning and the crackle and rumble of a great earthquake.

An angel appears at the grave. It has a fierce face, colored with streaks of fire like lightning. Its robes are white as snow. It rolls back the stone from the grave, revealing an empty cave with only a shroud and, separately, a headband, both lying on a stone slab. The angel pushes the stone completely clear of the entrance, enters the tomb and sits on the stone with a gesture of triumph.

The women are terrified and bow down and kneel and weep. They cover their faces and cry and pray. They lift up their faces and clasp their hands then raise their hands wide above their heads in silent prayer. They are distraught.

THE ANGEL OF THE TOMB: *(forcefully)*
Do not be frightened. What is there to fear?
You look for Jesus here in the tomb of death
But he is not here lying in the city of the dead
Long buried and forgotten in this garden.
(he waves his hand at the garden in general)
Why should you find him here in such a place?
Why should you seek the living among the dead?
Remember what he said to you in Galilee

That he, the Son of Man, would be betrayed
And given into the hands of wickedness
And crucified by hanging upon a tree
But on the third day after he was hanged
He would rise up.

MARY MAGDALENE: O let us then, let us look more closely.

The angel waves his hand to the tomb, Mary Magdalene approaches and looks and draws back.

MARY MAGDALENE:
(bitterly, crying and resentful)
Where is he then?
What have you done with him?
Please tell us?

ANGEL OF THE TOMB: Not I nor anyone has taken him. He is arisen from the dead. So be you happy. Praise him. He is alive.
He - is - alive *(slowly and gently)*
The greatest news that ever man has known.
Go tell his followers that he is alive.
Dead for three days – he has risen from the dead.
So do not be afraid - he is your friend.
The one who lives and has arisen from death.

MARY THE MOTHER: This news is good. He is alive. I must tell Peter and John.

Mary the Mother leaves. Salome and Mary Magdalene kneel, clasp their hands together beneath their chins, raise their faces up in joy and thanksgiving and quietness, whispering.

MARY MAGDALENE AND SALOME: He is alive.

They join hands and kneel left center.

MARY MAGDALENE: *(as Salome kneels beside her and repeats last line of each verse, either speaking or singing)*

Enter the Choir and sing or recite:
PRAISE TO JESUS
(Tune: Hyfrydol)

VERSE ONE:
   d - d   f - f   f   m   r - r
Praise to Jesus, bring him praises
   r   f   m   m   r - d - f
Praise the Lord for kindliness
   d - d   f   f   f - m   r - r
Praise the Lord for love and healing
   r   f   m   m   r   d   f
He will heal our minds and bless

VERSE ONE:

Praise to Jesus, bring him praises
Praise the Lord for kindliness
Praise the Lord for love and healing
He will heal our minds and bless

VERSE TWO:

Praise the Lord with trumpets blazing
Praise the Lord with harps that sing
Praise the Lord with drums and dancing
Praise the Lord with pipe and string

VERSE THREE:

Praise to Jesus, Praise to Jesus
All who have a voice to raise
Praise with music singing sweetly
Praise the Lord O give him praise

LET GOD BE KIND
(Tune: Ellacombe)

VERSE ONE:

d   f   m - r d   f   l₁ taw₁ d
Let God be kind and merciful

d r - m - f   f   m   *f*
O let the Lord's face shine

d   f   m - r d   f   l₁   taw₁ d
O let the Lord's face shine on us

  d   r m   f   f   m   *f*
And guard us with his smile

f - s l   s l taw   s   m - f s
 O   let salvation now be known

f - s l   s   l   taw   *s*
Let all men know God's ways

d   f   m - r d - f   l₁ taw₁   d
O let the people praise Him

  d r - m   f   f   m   *f*
Let all   the people praise

VERSE ONE:

Let God be kind and merciful
O let the Lord's face shine
O let the Lord's face shine on us
And guard us with his smile
O let salvation now be known
Let all men know God's ways
O let the people praise Him
Let all the people praise

VERSE TWO:
O let all nations now be glad
And sing for joy and mirth
For God will judge with righteousness
And fairness rule the earth
O let the people praise Him
Let all the people praise
The harvest then will flourish
And God our God will bless

VERSE THREE:
The Lord, our Lord will bless us
So let the clear harps ring
And all remotest nations
Will know the Lord and sing
O let salvation now be known
Let all men know God's ways
O let the people praise Him
Let all the people praise

Against the background of the red dawn sky, the shadowy silhouette of Jesus appears. The shadow is revealed slowly by lighting or spotlights at the top of the knoll, top, far right stage. The place where Jesus stands is hidden by bushes so that no actor appears in person - only a reflection.

Jesus is dressed in Eastern robes. His hair is long and he holds a shepherd's crook by his right side. His left hand is raised lightly in greeting.

Any effective technique may be used for the silhouette but the overall effect of this scene should be one of awe and joy and revelation (rather than terror or fear or surprise). Possible techniques include film or slide projection, the shadow of a live actor who is offstage or hidden from the audience, a projected shadow-image of a prop. The shadow-image may possibly be painted and lit by spotlight but preferably the shadow should have some movement. If it is static, then at least one other silhouette will be necessary, as the image changes dramatically at the end of the scene to a figure with outstretched arms.

The angel of the tomb continues to stand or kneel with the choir and now looks toward the shadow of Jesus and opens his arms wide and outward towards Jesus.

The Choir remains standing, front left, and look towards Jesus, each with one arm outstretched pointing to Jesus - as do Mary Magdalene and Salome.

<u>Curtain</u>

SCENE THREE
THE GOOD SHEPHERD

Scene - *The Same*
Enter Mary the Mother with Simon Peter, and John. *They first rush to the tomb, see that it is empty . . .*

JOHN: *(crying out)* You are right, Mother! There is nothing here but dead and dirty rags No man - no body, nothing.

> *Simon Peter, John and Mary the Mother see the shadow-image of Jesus and kneel, hands clasped together, prayerfully, left stage halfway between the choir and the tomb. All look at Jesus in joy. They are inspired, happy, trustful.*

SIMON PETER: *(speaking or singing)*

JESUS YOU ARE LIVING
(Tune: St. Patrick's Breastplate –
Be Thou My Vision)

VERSE ONE:

d - d   r   d l_1 s_1
Jesus, you are living

$s_1 l_1$ d   d   r m
We see you alive

r   r   r   r   m
How can this be Lord

s   l   s m s
Of one crucified?

l   l - t d^1 t   l   s m
You are the Sun rising

s   d t_1 l_1 s_1
Through skies that are red.

d   m   s   l s m
Death now is punished.

d m   r d d   d
Death is now dead

VERSE ONE:

Jesus, you are living
We see you alive
How can this be Lord
Of one crucified?
You are the Sun rising
Through skies that are red.
Death now is punished.
Death is now dead

VERSE TWO:
Will we all live, Lord
As you have lived through?
Can we all follow,
If we follow you?
Can we live also
If we trust in you?
Tell us and lead us
If this hope is true.

THE NARRATOR: *(echoing the words once spoken by Jesus, replying from off-stage, the shadow of Jesus does not speak)*
Jesus said, "I am the good shepherd
The good shepherd gives his life for the sheep
I am the resurrection and the life
He that believeth in me though he were dead
Yet shall he live. And whosoever
Liveth and believeth in me shall never die."

John and Simon Peter touch their clenched fists together with tense vigor. Mary Magdalene and Salome, in turn, embrace and kiss Mary the Mother.

JOHN: *(speaking or singing)*
Jesus you are living
We see you alive
How can this be Lord
Of one crucified?
You are the Sun rising
From skies that are red
Death now is punished
Death now is dead

VERSE THREE:
If one can live Lord
Then all may pass through
But we are not ready
Not fit to join you.
Wash us and lead us
Our one hope is true
For we must live in you
If we would live too.

These last eight lines are repeated by Simon Peter, the three women and the Choir, speaking or singing together.

NARRATOR: *(from off stage)*
O let you tell all nations to change their ways
And turn away from their greed and lies

And murderings
To look away from the tyrant and the drum
No more the sword of war and violent hatred
Yes, let them lead a new and better life
With fairness and with honesty
And with truth
And as you tell the good news to the world
You will be poor but you will give away
Your goods to those who are poorer still by far

JOHN:
I will trust in God for all my needs in life
For if he will meet my needs in afterlife
For endless ages, how will he neglect me
In these few years of witnessing and helping.

*Salome kneels left front and looks at Jesus. As Salome speaks or sings there is backing from Choir, who either join in the last line or repeat last two lines of **MY HUMBLE HEART**.*

MY HUMBLE HEART
(Tune: There is a Green Hill)

VERSE ONE:

d   r m   f   m   s   f-m r

My humble heart and hands and eyes

s   m d^1 t   l   s

Are not too high and grand

  r m f-f f m l   l-law

For I never act in great affairs

law l f   m r d

Too hard to understand

VERSE ONE:

My humble heart and hands and eyes
Are not too high and grand
For I never act in great affairs
Too hard to understand

VERSE TWO:

My soul is quiet well composed
At peace within my breast
Like a young child in its mother's arms
So is my mind at rest

VERSE THREE:

Like a young child in its mother's arms
My mind is now at ease
I am quite content to pray and trust
For all my daily needs.

(All in Refrain, speaking or singing)

VERSE FOUR:
We'll fish among the seas of men
To make the sick man whole
We'll throw the net of good new life
And harvest living souls.

NARRATOR: *(from offstage)*
Jesus said: I am the bread of life - he that cometh to me shall never hunger. Therefore, go you into all the world and publish this good news to every living creature.

The company is overjoyed and alive with inspiration. They raise their hands in joy. They briefly and silently bow heads and clasp hands in fragments of prayer, then stretch out legs and arms like the rays of the sun.

MARY THE MOTHER: *(kneeling center, looking at Jesus, singing or speaking the following verses)*

THE LIVING DOOR
(Tune: Bye and Bye We'll See the King)

VERSE ONE:

 m r d f m r d

Praise the Lord for eyes and ears

 r d t₁ l s f m

Praise the Lord for life's long years

 m r d f m r d

Praise the Lord for drying tears

 d r f m r d

His truth is great, so praise

 s₁ d - t₁ d - r m - m r - r r

God's truth is everlasting truth

 s₁ r - de r - m f - f m - m m

God's truth is everlasting truth

 d f - m f - s l - l s taw - taw

God's truth is everlasting truth

 taw l d₁ f taw l s f

So praise the Lord and sing always

VERSE ONE:

Praise the Lord for eyes and ears
Praise the Lord for life's long years
Praise the Lord for drying tears
His truth is great, so praise
God's truth is everlasting truth
God's truth is everlasting truth
God's truth is everlasting truth
So praise the Lord and sing always

VERSE TWO:
O Praise the Lord for bright new day
O Praise the Lord, all nations pray
O Praise the Lord, he is the way
His love is great, so praise
O Jesus is the Living Door
O tell the good news more and more
Go tell all creatures great and poor
Walk through him to the timeless shore

MARY MAGDALENE:
(speaking or singing)

REFRAIN:
Jesus is the Living Door
Jesus is the Living Door
Jesus is the Living Door
We walk with Him to live
O trust the Lord and live always
O trust the Lord and live always
O trust the Lord and live always
(repeat last line slowly)

Mary Magdalene stands beside Mary the Mother, center. Mary Magdalene speaks or sings:

THE RISEN ONE
(Tune: Old One Hundredth or
All People that On Earth Do Dwell)

VERSE ONE:

  d   d t_1 l_1 s_1 d r   m
All nations praise the Risen One
  m   m   m   r   d   f m r
Praise God and shout in joyfulness
  d   r   m   r d l_1 t_1 d
Serve him with happiness of heart
   s   m d   r   f   m   r   d
And follow in his steps of peace.

VERSE ONE:

All nations praise the Risen One
Praise God and shout in joyfulness
Serve him with happiness of heart
And follow in his steps of peace.

VERSE TWO:

For Jesus is the Risen One
Of fish and bird and seas and land
All creatures of the living world
God made and formed them with his hand.

VERSE THREE:

We are his sheep - the Risen One -
And we like sheep have walked astray
Enter new fields with thankfulness

O come into his streams and pray.
VERSE FOUR:
Give thanks and bless the Risen One
His healing kindness must live on.
We see the hills of endless life
All shining in this new-life dawn.

VERSE FIVE:
Give thanks and bless the Risen One
That where he goes, we may go too.
He has walked back from death and hell
And he will lead us safely through.

CHOIR: *(speaking or singing with support from the entire company, as before)*

THE GOOD SHEPHERD
(Tune: The 23rd Psalm)

VERSE ONE:
  d m f r   s f   r   d t_1 d
The Lord is my shepherd. He meets my needs
  m m r r   fe fe s
He gives me green fields to rest
  m m f m r f   f s   f m
He leads me beside the waters of peace
  m r f l   d t_1 d
My soul is made whole and blessed

VERSE ONE:

The Lord is my shepherd. He meets my needs
He gives me green fields to rest
He leads me beside the waters of peace
My soul is made whole and blessed

VERSE TWO:

With Him I do good for His name is Good
When valleys are dark and drear
And I must walk through the shadow of death
I never will walk with fear

VERSE THREE:

For you walk beside me in all of my ways
Your guidance and strength are here
You lay out a meal of blessings for me
That all who have doubts may see

VERSE FOUR:

You pour out the oil of good life on me
You pour it out more and more
Your goodness and mercy dwell with me now
And will do for evermore

NARRATOR: *(from offstage)*
Jesus said to his followers
"I am the door, by me if any man enter in,
He shall be saved"

And Jesus also said to all: "Follow me."
CHOIR: The Lord has risen up from the grave and He leads us

THE GOOD LORD IS OUR SHEPHERD

ALL:

f s   l - l   f   d   taw$_1$ l$_1$

The Good Lord is our shepherd

taw$_1$ d   f   f - f   f

He meets us in our need

　s   l   s   l   taw   d^1 d^1 l

He leads us by the streams of peace

d^1 taw   r   m   r   d

To fields where we may feed

　l   d^1 l   d^1 - d^1 taw - taw l

He brings the spring-time greenness

　l   f - f   r - r   taw

We sow the new-life seed

f   s   l - l   f   d - taw$_1$

Oh the Lord is still alive

l$_1$ taw$_1$ d   f

And He leads us

ALL:

The Good Lord is our shepherd
He meets us in our need
He leads us by the streams of peace
To fields where we may feed
He brings the spring-time greenness
We sow the new-life seed

Oh the Lord is still alive
And He leads us

All remain on stage, standing still, looking towards the silhouette of Jesus, which is now seen with arms outstretched in welcome to all.

Curtain
END OF PLAYSCRIPT

Soldiers for the Dawn

ABOUT THE PLAY

The Play is set out as a dialog spoken between two Roman guards at the tomb of Jesus.

They agreed between them:
The tomb was sealed!
The tomb was sealed and no one came to open it.
The prophet has arisen by himself.
This could mean life to us and to all men.
Why could I never see these things before?
I have always believed in nature but not in God.
A flower at dawning is my faith in God.
This garden which was dead just yesternight.
Is now alive with creatures of the dawn,
Where ferns and flowers hide the fleeing fox,
The birds and squirrels in the greening trees
Are chattering and eating as they gabble
And so it is, with our new faith and hope,
The resurrection of this prophet is like
The coming of the spring
Dead yesterday but now alive in Jesus.
Our prayer is that this faith so dead, so long
Will grow the greenery soon of gentler works
And clearer happier thoughts
Come through my mind.
Just as the spring must show itself in leaves.

Playscript

OUTLINE OF THE PLAY

SCENE ONE: The Garden of the Tomb
SCENE TWO: The Tomb Cracks
SCENE THREE: The Risen One

Two Roman Soldiers guard the tomb of Jesus Christ. They discuss life and religion and then witness the resurrection. Some justifications for the Christian faith are presented as unbelievers may be converted to Christ. The Resurrection is compared to the return of spring after winter.

PRODUCTION NOTES

One Act, One Set, Three Solo Singers and a Choir, to chant and sing. Three Scenes. This is a verse oratorio for those who like to think seriously about the Resurrection of Jesus Christ.

Creativity:

Good, but optional, opportunities for creative nature scenes with bird, beast or wind sound effects. Although music in chant or song is the main element of the oratorio, support from an organ or group is optional.

Music:

The Living Door, Jesus You are Living,
The Risen One, Watchmen in the Night,
Change Your Mind, When I Look Up,
Does Pain Remain, If You are Really There,
I Will Fly, O Come Where Songbirds Sing.

Stage Time: About 35-45 minutes

LIST OF CHARACTERS
Urelius   - a Guard at the Tomb
Virgilius - a Guard at the Tomb
A lead singer of the Choir.
An actor to present the shadow of Jesus.
The Choir of Creation to sing or chant –
as Angel of Death.
Black Robed Mourners in Scene One.
Moon and Stars in Scene Two.
Tree and Flowers in Scene Three.
Mary Magdalene to sing two choruses.

The two main elements in this possible oratorio are (a) verse, rhymed or unrhymed, which is suitable for Gregorian Chant and (b) ten songs or choruses to be sung as solo or choral pieces, in the usual style. The verse, rhymed or unrhymed, in the play can be chanted within the framework of the following melodies.

Music for Gregorian Chant:
Writing down the exact notes of Gregorian Chant is like writing down the exact notes of drum music. Technically, this is quite possible, indeed simple, but those who are familiar with either chant or drumming will always prefer to make their own interpretations based on a written melody. Therefore, the next section will present melodies suitable to be used as a basis for traditional ecclesiastical chant. This music is in addition to the ten melodies listed above, all of which are suitable for the attenuated or syncopated application necessary for chant.

CHANT 1:

d   m   m - m   r   m   s   s
d^1 l   s   l   d^1 l   s - s
d - d   m   m   m - r   m   s   *l*
s - s   m   r   d - d
s - s   d^1 d^1 - t   t   l   l
d^1 s   l - l - s   f - m   m   r - r
d - d - m   m   m   r   m   s   *l*
s - s   m   r   d - d
d - r   m   r   d
d   r   m   m - m - r   *d*

CHANT 2:

d r   m f m   f   s   f   r   taw$_1$ *d*   d   *d - d*
f s   l   *taw*   l   taw   *d taw*   l   taw   l   taw   *d^l*
d   r m   f   m f s   f m   f   m   f s
d r   m f   m   f   s   f   r   taw$_1$ *d*   d   *d - d*
d r m   f m   f   s f m   f   m   f s
d r m   f   m f   s   f   r taw$_1$ *d*   *d - d*

CHANT 3:

d   r - m   f   d taw_1 l_1 - f_1 - maw_1

f_1 l_1 - d taw_1 l_1 f_1 f_1 - *f_1*

d   r   m   f - d taw_1 - l_1 f_1 - maw_1

f_1 l_1 - d taw_1 - l_1 f_1 f_1 *f_1*

f   s - l   taw f maw r - taw_1 - law_1

f   s l   taw f s s l - l *taw*

d   r   m - f   d taw_1 l_1 - f_1 - maw_1

f_1 l_1 d taw_1 l_1 f_1 f_1 - *f_1*

f   s l taw - f maw - r - taw_1 law_1

f   s l taw f s s l - l *taw*

d   r   m   f   d - taw_1 - l_1 - f_1 - maw_1

f_1 l_1 d taw_1 l_1 f_1 f_1 - *f_1*

CHANT 4:

d f l s f f m r f r d

f l d^1 d^1 taw l s f f m f s

d f l l s f f m r f r d

f l - d^1 d^1 taw l d f m f s f

f r^1 r^1 r^1 taw d^1 r^1 d^1 f s l

l taw d^1 taw l l s f f - m f s

d f l l s f f m r f r d

f - l d^1 d^1 taw l d f m f s f

CHANT 5:
l fe r r m - fe s - m l
s m r - r de r
l r¹ r¹ t r¹ de¹ - l t
s m - m fe s - l
l - l r¹ t r¹ de¹ l t
s m m - fe s l
s - m r r m fe s m l
s m r r r r

CHANT 6:
m f s m - f - m r - d *m* r − r
m - f *s* - m f m r d l₁
m f *s* m f m r d *m* r r
s₁ l₁ d - d m r d l₁ s₁
m f s m f - m - r d m r − r
m - f s m f m r - d l₁
m - f s m f m r d m r − r
s₁ - l₁ d m r r - d l₁ s₁
m - f s m f m r d - m r r
m f s s - s m f - m r d l₁
m - f s - m m f m r d m r r
s₁ l₁ d m r - d l₁ s₁

SCENE ONE
THE GARDEN OF THE TOMB

Time: The pre-dawn twilight.

The crucifixion appears in shadow silhouette on the left stage side drop, three crosses, three persons. It is lit clearly at first, then the shadows of the crucifixion gradually disappear as some light partially reveals the scene of the tomb and the garden.

The two guards, Urelius and Virgilius, are seen standing outside the burial cave in front of the stone that seals it. They are dressed as Romans in short tunic, curved helmets and with short broad swords in hand, sandals on feet. Uneasily, they pace back and forth outside the tomb.

VIRGILIUS: This place terrifies me. I need to pray.

URELIUS: *(shakes his head)* That'll do a lot of good, I don't think. *(Virgil looks shocked)* O pray all you like but keep your eyes open.

Virgilius prays silently.

URELIUS: Well Virgil,
I hope you have made yourself feel better
After that demonstration of fear and escape.
I just hope that you don't think
You've achieved something
That you've won over God to be on our side
And then go and get careless and fall asleep,
Or do something silly
And self-confident like that.
At least not without telling me
So that I can be sure
To stay doubly aware.
(aside, casually) What was that noise?

VIRGILIUS: One thing is certain.

URELIUS: What's that?

VIRGILIUS:
Neither you nor I
Will get good sleep tonight.

URELIUS:
But maybe later we can watch in turns,
Even if one of us is sleeping.

VIRGILIUS:
I've served 20 years as a guard
And watchman and battle warrior.
I've never felt so uneasy about a place.
This place is shivery.
It's unnatural, spooky.
It's filled with the smell of death.
It's <u>somehow</u> alive and watching us
And yet I've never known
A place as deadly quiet.
(He points to the tomb)
This one was a strange one - a prophet
He makes me uneasy.
Not that we're doing him any harm but still
I feel somehow as if
We're working against him.

URELIUS: How?
We are only trying to make sure
That his body is not snatched.
What's wrong with that?

VIRGILIUS: Oh nothing.
That's fine but the ones who hired us
Were the ones who had him hanged.
I feel bad about that.

URELIUS: He's just a body to guard
Until he becomes so stinking
That no one would want to steal him.

VIRGILIUS:
Then how do you explain the storm?

URELIUS: What storm?

VIRGILIUS: Well, the storm . .
earthquake
The darkness over the earth
When he was hanged.
The rumbling in the rocks
The black tremors in the earth
What do you call this?
If it was not a storm, then what was it?

URELIUS: It was just bad weather.

VIRGILIUS: Just like that - just by
chance?

URELIUS:
I wouldn't say that such a wild upheaval
Was just by chance
At the exact time of his death.

VIRGILIUS: So it was God at work.
You admit it. God was angry.

URELIUS:
I wouldn't put it like that . .
Let me explain, my friend.
Death - the death of anyone or any creature
Is a terrible thing
Unnatural death
Murder, execution, accident, whatever,
Blasts a hole in the universe.
Nature - the natural world
Is all one - is wounded
The fields, the trees, the hills, the rocks
Cry out against it.

VIRGILIUS: Against <u>any</u> unnatural death.

URELIUS: Yes - for sure,
You've been a soldier for 20 years
And I for 40.
Have you ever known,
Have you ever, ever, known
A day of execution to be
A bright, shining, happy day?

VIRGILIUS: Well no . . but not 3 hours
Of darkness and earthquake.

URELIUS: Never mind that.
I'm trying to make a point.
Do you ever recall
A good day for a crucifixion?

VIRGILIUS: No, No I don't really.   Now
you come to mention it.   Seems like it was
mostly a cloudy and dull day.

URELIUS: *(as one scoring a point)*
Exactly, and this prophet's death
Is no different -
Except that the earth and sun and waters
Seemed to cringe and weep
And cry out more than usual –
I don't know why.
Maybe he was a good man
Who did not deserve to die.
I don't know.
But I do know that no day is
A good day for a hanging.
Nature screams out in pain against it.
It's a natural thing.
Don't you understand?
It's got nothing to do with gods

Or the supernatural.
Nature, the earth, seems to work
In harmony with
All living creatures,
Including us humans - understand?

VIRGILIUS: *(shakes his head)*
There's more to it.
There must be a guiding hand behind it all.

CHANGE YOUR MIND
Sung: Slow and Pleading

VERSE ONE:
f s   l - l   f   d   taw₁ l₁
Still, do you doubt the teaching
taw₁ d   f   f - f   f
Of those who gladly tell?
  s l   s   l   taw   dˡ dˡ   l dˡ
Maybe your prayers have not been answered,
taw   r   m   r   d
Life not gone so well?
  l   dˡ l   dˡ - dˡ   taw - taw   l
Or do you doubt the songs of hope
  l   f - f   r - r   taw
That ring from many a bell?
f s   l - l   f   d   taw₁
Then pray to find the way
  l₁   taw₁   d f
Change your mind.

VERSE ONE:

Still, do you doubt the teaching
of those who gladly tell?
Maybe your prayers have not been answered,
life not gone so well?
Or do you doubt the songs of hope
that ring from many a bell?
Then pray to find the way
Change your mind.

VERSE TWO:

O can you find no peace
after searching high and low?
Do you believe that this short life
is all that we can know?
That after we have died
there is no place else to go?
O pray to find the way
Change your mind.

VERSE THREE:

Do you believe there is
no heaven, no eternal plan?
Do you not see in nature
the work of one great hand?
Don't you know that all the sorrow
in this world is made by man?
Think it over one more time
And pray to find the way
Change your mind.

URELIUS:

Look, you agree that it is a strange fact
That when a hanging is to take place,
The weather is most always dull and cloudy.
This fact has been seen in all times
And in all places
And all across the world. The reason is
We - everyone - the creatures of the earth
Have grown out of the soil
And the soil out of the waters. So why should we
not all be part of each other?
Everything - all creatures and all living
Trees and fields and herbs - are part of one
Great family earth and why
Should not one part
Of that great family not cry out in pain
If some one part is to die before due time?

VIRGILIUS:

Well, I can surely agree with all that if
You just can see that a Great Creator must
Have made all living things together work
In harmony.

URELIUS:

It just so happens naturally
Without "Big God"
Without a guide or a "Great Spirit"

Directing it.
That's my belief. Nature is God. That's it.
And my ideas are based on facts
Just as we see them
Not on imaginations that we can't see.

WHEN I LOOK UP

f s l - l   f   d taw_1 l_1
When I look up and wonder
taw_1 d   f   f - f   f
What is there, there to find?
s   l   s l   taw $d^1 d^1$ l
Is anything up yonder
d^1 taw r   m   r   d
But discords of the mind?
l d^1 l d^1 - d^1 taw - taw l
Is there a faithful singer
l   f - f   r - r   taw
Who sings all tunes combined?
f   s l - l   d taw_1 l_1
 A coordinated ringer
taw_1 d   f   f   f   f
Of bells that blend in mind?

VIRGILIUS:
I know just what you mean.
But yet this place
Is somehow frightening and unnatural.
It's strange and alive and yet
As quiet as the grave.

I seem to sense great spiritual powers,
Both good and evil,
Hovering in the air over this garden.

URELIUS:
It's all to do with nature - nothing at all
To do with God or the Devil. All these beliefs
Are in your mind. See, you are quite upset
That a harmless preacher was executed.
That's your own feeling only . .
Don't you see it . . .?
Just your own feelings of upset
And hurt and horror.
Maybe you're right, I don't know
But I do know
It's nothing to do with God.
It's all about DEATH.
And that's it - Death is the name of the game.

VIRGILIUS:
I've seen enough death . . red death in battle,
Death for stealing, lying
And cheating in small amounts.
Now death has come for preaching
And healing the sick.
There's no death penalty for grabbing land
Or gathering taxes

From the poor and hungry.
Or what of wealth built up
From the booty of war?

URELIUS: As for this prophet . . .
He was taking business away
From orthodox preachers,
And recognized healers and that's
A serious offense, you know.

VIRGILIUS:
Maybe but what's next - death for anything
That takes a little power away from
priests?

URELIUS:
There's death for us if
The body is stolen, for sure.
I'll guard it with my life.
My life is gone if that poor body is snatched.

> **Enter Choir** (dressed as mourners
> in black robes and hoods), from stage
> right. Angel of Death and others
> stand center front and address the
> Roman Soldiers.

Stop and think we beg you
There's nothing in this world
But death and things
That lead to death.
It's all a delusion, surely the real world
Is the next one.
A world cannot be real and true when people
Who have no substance in themselves,
Drab people
Of no true worth, are given all - wealth, land,
And honor
Given all by the leaders of the world.
These things must be bad dreams
Give us the reality
Of the next world that God
Has promised man.
Aye, only God's true
And promised world is real -
All else, all this sad sickness and decay,
All else is suffering madness and delusion.
Stop and think we pray you.

Choir leaves right.

URELIUS:
There is no other world, Virgilius, friend,
This is all you get. Once you are dead,
You're gone and that is it. Nobody rises,

No one returns from the shadowy world
Of the dead.
That's just what they tell you to get you
To do the things that they want.
It's cheaper than wages.
Do a good job and, well
We won't exactly pay you,
No extra really
But you'll surely go to heaven when you die.
No pie now, we're sorry to admit
But plenty of pie in the sky,
Some plum sweet day.

He ruminates, muttering to himself

Don't help yourself to anything of mine,
For if I catch you
I'll see that you are punished.
But whether we catch you or not,
Good God will get you
And punish you by putting you in Hell
After you die.
Some chance.
To Virgilius
Don't you see that it's all a fairy tale
To turn you into a good obedient slave
So that the cunning frauds
And liars and thieves,

Who run this world,
Can carry on destroying us
And robbing us and sending us to war
To guard their treasures
And defend their lives.

VIRGILIUS:
(calmly) That's not the whole truth.
Listen, Urelius,
I'm sure you're right that the name
Of God has been taken in vain
By greedy men to justify their greed
But God is real and there is a life beyond life.
I have heard tales
Of the earthy paradise - Elysian
Some have called it,
A land far to the west,
It rises high in the sky . . .
(He raises hands in awe)
Far distant - it touches
The path of the moon . . .
(with enthusiasm)
Waters of the flood did not destroy it . . .
See over there - the moon.

<u>Curtain</u>

SCENE TWO
THE TOMB CRACKS

The Same: **Enter from right, Choir** *led by the moon, with the stars following. The Moon and Stars Choir of Creation gather front center to recite or sing. All wear white robes and headwear, either mid-Eastern style or other. The jacket of the moon is set with moons and pale yellow rays. The jackets of the stars is set with silver stars and sequins.*

The last to enter is the sun, with headdress like a sunflower whose white jacket is covered in symbols of the sun in full ray. Later, only jacket and headwear will need to be changed for transformation to trees and flowers.

CHOIR:
Beware of tales. There are many tragic tales
Tales, tales and songs . . weak lies,
And lies well lied
Leading to lives ruined in the ravages of war.
Innocents slaughtered out of greed
And fear and hate.
There are too many tales

And songs of battles far
And paradises for the warriors
Who have died.
(quickly and with bitterness)
Beware of tales.
There are too many tragic longings
And men are driven to their doom by songs.
There are songs too sad for singing.
There are tales too true to tell.
As lands too bleak and barren
For bird or man to dwell.
There are tales that hold no whispering
Of wisdom for the way
And songs too terrible and sad
For any harp or horn to play.
Tales that can never help escape
Or show the soul a place to hide,
Tales that can only feed a fear
A terror growing deep inside,
Tales that can hold no hope of heaven
No fear of hell or any thing.
Like seas too steep and deep to sail in
There are songs too sad to sing.
For life is a random lottery.
Success is as elusive as moon beams.
Those who seek truth
Must always stand aside

Locked in the loneliness of dreams.
For those who once thought to feast
And drink their fill
From the glass of gladness
Generously filled up
Would now drink greedily
The dregs that spill
From any cup.

Choir *leaves stage, left.*

VIRGILIUS:
But my friend there are good things
that can happen too . . .
You never can be sure when we will find
A great store of wealth
Or get promotion in battle.

URELIUS: *(morosely)* Ah no, my friend,
This is one miserable assignment.
A blacker night I have never known.
What did I do wrong as a young man?
Where did I stray from the way of success?
To end up in a place like this
Guarding the dead from the damned
In a chilly, obscure old garden.
Why am I not in command of my own ship?
Riding the green mountains

Of the sea to victory.
Aye, it seems like a long time
Since I was happy.

VIRGILIUS: Yes,

DOES PAIN REMAIN?

Sung: Slow and Sad

VERSE ONE:

f   s   l - l   f   d   taw$_1$ l$_1$

When friend betrays and hinders

taw$_1$ d   f   f - f   f

And we forgive the friend

s   l   s   l   taw   d^1 d^1 l

Why still does memory linger

d^1 taw   r   m   r   d

And pain remain in mind?

l   d^1 d^1 l   d^1 taw - taw   l

With heart burned to a   cinder

l   f - f   r - r   taw

We leave old loves behind

f   s   l - l   f   d   taw$_1$ l$_1$

Ah, why does memory linger

taw$_1$ d   f   f   f   f

And pain remain in mind?

VERSE ONE:
When friend betrays and hinders
And we forgive the friend
Why still does memory linger
And pain remain in mind?
With heart burned to a cinder
We leave old loves behind
Ah, why does memory linger
And pain remain in mind?

VERSE TWO:
When lands flame up like tinder
New peaceful fields we find
So why does memory linger?
Must pain remain in mind?
When points that Mighty Finger
Across the tide of time
Even there, does memory linger?
Does pain remain in mind?

The life of a soldier can be
A hard and bitter one
(humbly)
The profession of blood is cruel and unkind.
But we're not the only ones
The life of a prophet
Is also hard or the life of anyone

Who opposes the inexorable powers that be.
Like this one here for instance
Not a nice end.

URELIUS: Who?

VIRGILIUS: The one in here *(pointing to the tomb)*

URELIUS: *(a little uneasy)*
Oh yes, that one . . .
Well most likely he was just a trickster,
Fooling people
Making them believe that they were healed.

VIRGILIUS: *(with light irony)* Surely not.
Making blind people believe
That they could see . . ?
Now I . . I see - that's quite a trick,
Indeed *(laughs briefly)*

URELIUS:
Well . . you just can't believe
All that you hear.
You need the proof of what is said.
Where is the proof?

See, I'm not trying to attack
Your beliefs, Virgilius,
I'm just trying to keep our thinking clear.
It's bad enough that we
Could get killed by a bunch
Of body-snatching fanatics.
It's bad enough all this -
Our low wages and this dark
And miserable task.
This spookiness and all this deadly silence.
(looking around suddenly)
(aside: Why are there no animal noises
here? It's strange.)

Yes, all this is bad enough
Without your doubts
Confusing us both about life
After death and such. *(he shivers and prays)*

IF YOU ARE REALLY THERE

f   s   l-l   f   d   taw₁   l₁
If you are really there, god
taw₁   d   f   f-f   f
Please make my faith to grow
s   l   s   l   taw   d¹   l
And prove that you are there, god,
d¹   d¹   taw   r   m   r   d
In a way that I will know.

(pleadingly)
Come on, my friend,
Let's try to bear up a little.

VIRGILIUS: *(shaking his head sadly)*
I'm sorry friend, really I'm sorry,
But death, as you said, is what this place
Is all about.
The smell of death lingers here
Like the smell of after-battle,
Strong and damp with blood
And filth and sickness.
The smell of hatred –
The worst smell in the world.

URELIUS:
It'll not be so bad when
The dead one's followers anoint him.
They'll be here at the first light of dawn
I dare say . . .
He had a multitude of followers
At one time . . .
There must be a few left still,
Who will anoint him.

VIRGILIUS:
Yes, I hope so *(uneasily he cocks an ear)*
But listen . . look . . .

URELIUS: Yes, Virgil.

VIRGILIUS: Look,
This whole garden is spooky
And . . I thought . . .
No it couldn't be . . .

URELIUS: You thought what . . tell it,
Virgil.

VIRGILIUS:
I thought I heard a sound coming
From the grave.
The tomb . . it seemed to groan.
It sent long shivers
In a tingling down my spine.

URELIUS: *(incredulous)*
A noise through all that solid,
Carved out stone?
No animal could get in there . . .
It's quite impossible.

VIRGILIUS: *(relieved)* No. You're right . .
My mind is playing tricks on me.
It's all this deadly silence that destroys
My piece of mind more
Than the screams of battle

Or the turmoil of war. Why is it so still?

URELIUS: *(uncertainly)*
I told you. Animals and birds and such
Are well . . sensitive to death
Or imminent destruction.
They surely sense it. It's nothing miraculous,
It is their natural instinct.

VIRGILIUS: *(fearfully looking around)*
But what about
The blackness that came
Over the whole disjointed earth
When this man died?
Do you mean that earth
And sky was being sensitive
To the death of one ordinary human person,
That this is just a natural thing to happen,
That the Creator of Earth had nothing
At all to do with it?

URELIUS: Virgil,
I do not claim
To understand these things.
From every life-view and in every detail
I am trying to give us courage
To live our lives

To lighten our load on life's
Long loathsome way
By trying to set us free from superstition.
Yes, free from fear of the "great powers
Of the universe."
(he shivers)

Suppose for the sake of argument
That these great powers
Do really exist for evil works and good,
What can we do about it?
Fear them as you do?
Or, like me,
To try to banish them, brush them aside
And set our spirits free from
The strangling fears.
It's a hard life to be a professional soldier.
I don't need fear. Fear I can live without.
Fear comes at me like a broad
Warrior with sword
Fear is a phalanx facing me
Fear is a chariot driven by
A full armored warrior
Bearing down on us
But I don't want that, No.

VIRGILIUS:
It's not the warrior I fear, it's this . . .

URELIUS: *(puzzled)* This what?

VIRGILIUS:
This tomb . . this cave . . this garden . .
This man . . this Prophet.

Enter the Choir, *(in contrast) lightly and pleasantly led by the Moon and Stars (right stage). The Moon addresses and approaches the guards.*

MOON:
It is the darkest hour before the dawn.
Please do not be afraid.
You have nothing to fear.
You have done no wrong.
You are here to do a job -
Protect this tomb - that is a good
And worthy thing.
You will be witnesses that no legerdemain,
No trickery took place tonight. Be happy
That you are witnesses to the death of death
The only truthful story that ever was known
Of life and death and rising up
From the dead.

WATCHMEN IN THE NIGHT
(Tune: O for a Thousand Tongues or Lyngham)

VERSE ONE:

d   m   f   s-l-s-f-m   f   m   d   r   t$_1$ *d*

O bless the Lord of Life all you who serve so well

m   f   m   r   d   r

As watchmen in the night

r   m-r-m   f   s l   s fe *s*

As witnesses and watchmen in the night

   s   s   s   m r   d   m   f   m   r   d   r

Searching for truth in what you hear and see and know

s$_1$ d   r   m

Until the morn

 d f f   f f   *m*

Until the morning light

m r   r   r-m-f-r   s

Until the morning light

s l   s   f m   r r   *d*

Until the truthful morning light

VERSE ONE:

O bless the Lord of Life all you who serve so well
As watchmen in the night
As witnesses and watchmen in the night
Searching for truth in what you hear and see and know
Until the morn
Until the morning light
Until the morning light
Until the truthful morning light

VERSE TWO:
O bless the Lord of Life all you who serve so well
As watchmen for the day
As witnesses and watchmen for the day
Guarding the poor and weak from robbers and from wrong
Lift up your hands
Lift up your hands to pray
Lift up your hands to pray
Lift up your faithful hands to pray

VERSE THREE:
And may the Lord of Life who made the earth and skies
Who set the heavens above
Who scattered all the stars in heaven up above
Help the true watchman live for faithfulness and truth
And bless you now
And bless you now with love
And bless you now with love
And bless the watchman now with love

Choir leave left stage.

<u>Curtain</u>

SCENE THREE
THE RISEN ONE

The Same. Dawn, a red orange light is beginning to lighten the sky. The two soldiers are pacing up and down in front of the tomb.

URELIUS:
The sun arises from his sleep. The dawn.
Yawns and long beams of
Steamy misted light.
Pick out the sights and smells
Of a spring morning.

VIRGILIUS: Ah . . .
The daylight comes to drive away the ghosts.
Last night was the dreariest death-watch
In the world.

The Shadow of Jesus appears walking across the stage and tomb. The guards see that the tomb is empty.
The guards are speechless and draw back in fear, their right-handed swords drawn but held back and pointing downwards as fear drives them back,

with their left hands drawn across their faces to shield them from the brightness and supernatural power of the appearance of Jesus.

Enter the choir of creation *- front left - as trees and flowers, wearing white jackets with tree and flower design. One wears a sunflower headdress, some with flowers in hair, green leaves on headdress and gowns. Guards still stand like frozen statues in martial stance to right of tomb, swords drawn and pointed, slightly crouched, as though half expecting an attack, their own hands thrown wide for balance. The Choir of Creation joins them. They all look towards the empty tomb.*

CHOIR:
Jesus the Savior has arisen -
Just as He said
He would arise like flowers after rain
(with forcefulness)
He would arise out from the grave
Just as He said
And he will one day raise the dead to life

All who believed in him, he will raise up
Setting them free from death for evermore
All who believed him and followed him
Would rise to live forever at the last day

The guards are still distraught, draw back in terror, stare into the empty tomb.

URELIUS: *(in a daze, still not understanding)*
The body is gone. We are as good as dead.
They have snatched it. We have failed.
They will destroy us. Let me end it now.
(he points his sword as though to kill himself)

VIRGILIUS:
(holding back the sword arm of Urelius)
The tomb was sealed!
The tomb was sealed
And no one came to open it.
Can't you see?
The prophet has arisen by himself!
You said yourself that truly
No creature could have entered
Through that stone.

URELIUS: *(dazed)* You're right!
What does this mean?

VIRGILIUS: *(slowly, thinking)*
The prophet has arisen by himself.
This could mean life to us and to all men.

JESUS YOU ARE LIVING
(Tune: St. Patrick's Breastplate –
Be Thou My Vision)

VERSE ONE:
d - d   r   d l_1 s_1
Jesus, you are living
$s_1 l_1$ d   d   r m
We see you alive
r   r   r   r   m
How can this be Lord
s   l   s m s
Of one crucified?
l   l - t d^1 t   l   s m
You are the Sun rising
s   d t_1 l_1 s_1
Through skies that are red.
d   m s   l s m
Death now is punished.
d m r d d   d
Death is now dead

VERSE ONE:
Jesus, you are living
We see you alive
How can this be Lord
Of one crucified?
You are the Sun rising
Through skies that are red.
Death now is punished.
Death is now dead

VERSE TWO:
Will we all live, Lord
As you have lived through?
Can we all follow,
If we follow you?
Can we live also
If we trust in you?
Tell us and lead us
If this hope is true.

Urelius is thoughtful. He lowers his sword. He shakes his head. He covers his face with his left hand, presses his forehead with his fists, raises his head.

The guards are gradually unfrozen. They are amazed but joyful. They kneel and look at the shadow of Jesus.

VIRGILIUS:
If you can live, Lord
Then why not we too?
We ordinary men too - not prophets
Can we be resurrected?
Surely we also can be raised up after
We die
For we believe in you.

URELIUS:
But many will never believe
That Jesus is arisen,
They will say that we are liars or deceived,
We were mistaken after a sleepless night,
Yes, we were bribed to allow the body
To be stolen
Or tricked by a flickering
Of the early morning light,
Or it all was an illusion of the eyes
Performed by tricksters.
Yet it is true the Prophet is alive.

VIRGILIUS SINGS:

THE FLYING SONG

VERSE ONE:

d¹ l f f-m f r taw₁ d
I will fly along the song-bird's sky
 d r m f s l-taw s d¹
Swooping around, a jovial flyer
d¹ d¹ l f f-m f r taw₁ d
To all I know below, I'll call goodbye.
 d r m f-l r s m f
While the small people cling - I will fly.
 d f m f s l-taw d¹
I'll smile to see their creeping ways
 r¹ d¹ d¹ l f s l-d¹ taw l-s
As I climb and rise and circle up higher
 d¹ l f f m f r-taw₁ d
I will swing and sing of winging days
 d r-m f l r s m f
While above all things I, I will fly.

VERSE ONE:

 I will fly along the song-bird's sky
Swooping around, a jovial flyer
To all I know below, I'll call goodbye.
While the small people cling - I will fly.
I'll smile to see their creeping ways
As I climb and rise and circle up higher
I will swing and sing of winging days
While above all things I, I will fly.

VERSE TWO:

High over clouds and rains I'll fly
Far above the fear and lying
A free-bird strong in song and mirth, I'll cry.
From the sad sigh of earth - I will fly
Up where the air is new and true
Through a glad sky where no-one is pining or dying
I will glide in flight across the blue
But above all things I, I will fly.

VIRGILIUS:

What you have said is true Urelius, yet
If they do not believe
When we first tell them,
Later, when they see that truly we believe,
Many and many will believe also,
What man has reason to defend illusion
Or fraud or anything at all uncertain?
Nevertheless, we will tell
The good news humbly and in joy.
Let it be known to every living creature
That Jesus is Lord of a path to life,
A resurrection way.
Forces of fate and hate
And all that we feared by firelight
Now fade into the brightness of his day.

Urelius stands, raises his sword then sheaths it.

The sound of birds chattering, singing and rustling is heard, breezes blow. The flowers enter, led by the tree.

LEADER OF CHOIR: *(the tree)*
Why could you never see these things before?
You have always believed in nature
But not in God.
A flower at dawning is your faith in God.
This garden which was dead just yesternight.
Is now alive with creatures of the dawn,
Where ferns and flowers hide the fleeing fox,
The birds and squirrels in the greening trees
Are chattering and eating as they gabble
And so it is, with man's new faith and hope,
Dead yesterday but now alive in Jesus.
Our prayer is that this faith so dead, so long
Will grow the greenery soon of gentler works
And clearer happier thoughts
Come through your mind.
Just as the spring must show itself in leaves
So must your faith now grow
The leaves of works
Pleasing to God and to believers also.
There is no spring without the

Springtime greenery.
There can be no true faith without true works
So let your work be pleasing to the Lord.
And let the good news be known
To every creature.

Optional - sounds of the garden in the background until the end of the play.

Enter Mary Magdalene and Sings – THE RISEN ONE and THE CALLING ANGEL'S SONG.

THE RISEN ONE
(Tune: Old One Hundredth <u>or</u> All People that On Earth Do Dwell)

VERSE ONE:
d   d t₁   l₁   s₁   d r   m
All nations praise the Risen One
m   m   m   r   d   f m r
Praise God and shout in joyfulness
d   r   m   r d l₁   t₁   d
Serve him with happiness of heart
s   m d   r   f   m   r   d
And follow in his steps of peace.

VERSE ONE:

All nations praise the Risen One
Praise God and shout in joyfulness
Serve him with happiness of heart
And follow in his steps of peace.

VERSE TWO:

For Jesus is the Risen One
Of fish and bird and seas and land
All creatures of the living world
God made and formed them with his hand.

VERSE THREE:

We are his sheep - the Risen One -
And we like sheep have walked astray
Enter new fields with thankfulness
O come into his streams and pray.

VERSE FOUR:

Give thanks and bless the Risen One
His healing kindness must live on.
We see the hills of endless life
All shining in this new-life dawn.

VERSE FIVE:

Give thanks and bless the Risen One
That where he goes, we may go too.
He has walked back from death and hell
And he will lead us safely through.

Mary and the rest of the Choir of Creation: (in unison)

THE CALLING ANGEL'S SONG - ALONG THAT SILVER SHORE
Sung: Sweetly and Plaintively

VERSE ONE:

d - d   f   d   f - s   l   l taw taw - taw d^1

O come where song birds sing and all the wild woods

taw l taw l f *s*

are ringing

d^1 - taw   l - l   l - f   *s*

Where fragrant flowers sway

d^1 - taw   l   f   f - s   l - s

O   come, O come away

d - d   f   s   l taw - l   s   f - m   *f*

Where slow songs glide along that silver shore

REFRAIN:

s   l   s   m   d   d - r   m

Blow, blow, so free the breezes flow

d   d   s$_1$ d   r   m   m   f   s   r

To soothe the eyes with airs so soft and low

s - s   s   s - s - s   m   f

Over there is a light of dawn

s   f - m   d   d - r - m   r

With a flame that   lingers on

s$_1$ - s$_1$ d   r - m f - r   r   d t$_1$ d

Dreams come alive along that silver shore

VERSE ONE:

O come where song birds sing
and all the wild woods are ringing
Where fragrant flowers sway
O come, O come away
Where slow songs glide along that silver shore

REFRAIN:

Blow, blow, so free the breezes flow
To soothe the eyes with airs so soft and low
Over there is a light of dawn
With a flame that lingers on
Dreams come alive along that silver shore

VERSE TWO:

O hear the streamlets sigh and the waterfalls a-crying
There the dark-red honeys glow
And the sweetening vinelets grow
For wines are deep along that silver shore

FLOWERS:

We are the lilies of the fields of spring
The flowers in the garden of the rain.
The mighty laughing spirit of creation
Sprays us with showers kindler than a breeze
But wetter than the mountains of the ocean.
We live, we grow, we jump,

We show our beauty
If you have faith in God, have love for us,
Do not destroy us for no life-need reason,
Be gentle with us, only let us live
As we help you to live. Let us be friends
As you help us to grow
Let us be friends.

*All the sounds of the garden are still
in the background.*

THE CHOIR OF CREATION: *(in unison)*
So water us and garden us and grow us
And we will send the rainfall back to you
And the rain will fall upon
Your favorite meadow
And the dying flowers will look up anew.

Lord, this is a message of hope
For all creation
So, truly let each creature hear the good news
Of resurrection and re-birth in you
For surely all will choose to live in you, Lord,
Rather than choose to die in self-destruction.
Let each earth-walker
And each water-swimmer
Let each air-flyer, have its own small voice.
Let every creature have its own

Place in safety,
Let all the greenery be watered
And looked after
Let all the waters of rivers and seas be loved,
Let every creature's place
And unique-featured face
Be loved by others,
And let this be, Lord, that we all may live.
Lord, let all your creatures help
The helpless one
And heal and hear each other. And let not
The trees and the flowers and
The waters be destroyed
By wars of greed and lies. Let us hear truth
And listen carefully to each other's voice.
Even the faintest.
Hear the clear rejoice
Of the small song bird
Why is it wasted away
By the wail of the world?
Who knows what gold or silver message
Each silent cry could give
If only each small voice could speak
And each small message live?
Perhaps some waters in a lost well
Could tell
A secret tale of toil and prospering

In the littler places where men dwell and sing
If only each small bell
Could knell
Its own clear spell
And quell
The dreary din of selfish scream and yell.
If only each small bird
Could make its message heard
Above the wordless words that flow
From empty minds that cannot know
And empty souls that cannot feel
If only each small bell could knell
What singing would be heard?
If only each small bell could peal
What wisdom would be shared?

Mary Sings **THE LIVING DOOR.**

THE LIVING DOOR
(Tune: Bye and Bye We'll See the King)

VERSE ONE:

m   r   d f   m   r   d

Praise the Lord for eyes and ears

r   d t_1 l s   f   m

Praise the Lord for life's long years

m   r   d f   m r   d

Praise the Lord for drying tears

d   r   f   m   r   d

His truth is great, so praise

s_1 d - t_1 d - r m - m r - r   r

God's truth is   everlasting truth

s_1 r - de r - m f - f m - m   m

God's truth is   everlasting truth

d   f - m f - s l - l s taw - taw

God's truth is everlasting truth

taw l d_1 f taw l   s f

So praise the Lord and sing always

VERSE ONE:

Praise the Lord for eyes and ears
Praise the Lord for life's long years
Praise the Lord for drying tears
His truth is great, so praise
God's truth is everlasting truth
God's truth is everlasting truth
God's truth is everlasting truth
So praise the Lord and sing always

VERSE TWO:
O Praise the Lord for bright new day
O Praise the Lord, all nations pray
O Praise the Lord, he is the way
His love is great, so praise
O Jesus is the Living Door
O tell the good news more and more
Go tell all creatures great or poor
Walk through him to the timeless shore

MARY MAGDALENE:
(chanting or singing)

REFRAIN:
Jesus is the Living Door
Jesus is the Living Door
Jesus is the Living Door
We walk with Him to live
O trust the Lord and live always
O trust the Lord and live always
O trust the Lord and live always
(repeat last line slowly)

Curtain
END OF PLAYSCRIPT

The Old Tramp and Easter

ABOUT THE PLAY

It was dawn on a springtime Easter morning when an Old Tramp walked up a hillside. He sat down, closed his eyes and had a vision of St. Paul. St. Paul told the Tramp how he met Jesus. Then the Tramp fell half asleep.

Later, he had a visit from the Sunflower. "I am the flower of the sun. Each night I sleep and each morning I awake, just as the sun goes down each night and rises again each morning. Sleeping and waking, death followed by life. This is the way of the earth. One day my seed will fall into the earth and die in the winter. Then when the rains of spring come and water the seed, it will arise to life again. Winter and spring, that is the cycle of the earth. So many things die in the winter and then rise up to life again in the spring."

As the Sunflower floated away, a Butterfly winged closer. "I am the Butterfly. A little while ago I was an old caterpillar that died and then came alive again as a butterfly. " Then a Crow, a Sparrow and a Dove chirped along as messengers of the spring. All spoke together, "We bring the message of the good news of the spring. Out we go with our good words and fly and fly and fly."

They gradually moved away from the Tramp, who called out to them. "Goodbye, you've helped me to understand things that were not clear."

Later, the Tramp was sleeping on the hillside as Paul again stood at the crest of the hill.

Paul spoke, "Jesus said: 'I am the door, by me if any man enter in he shall be saved.' Goodbye, Old Tramp. Remember my story and each Easter morning remember to come to this hillside to enjoy the spring and to remember the story of Jesus."

Paul threw a small silver coin to near where the Tramp was sleeping then left suddenly, as one disappearing into the thin air.

The Tramp was slightly aroused by the fall of the coin. He awakened mystified and asked himself, "I must have been dreaming. It must have been a story I learnt in childhood somehow come back to me."

Then he looked into the distance wistfully and remembered, "Look to the earth as a pattern of life and then look to God to give us a spring . . a new life after death to those who follow Jesus. What a good sermon for Easter. And, funny thing, I didn't even have to go to church. It's all here in the woods. The trees are a chapter. The birds are words. The flies and bees are the commas and dots. The skies are the pages. I can read it all in God's great book of creation."

The Tramp was now sitting up, going over the Easter story in his head, nodding to himself and muttering and looking at his Roman coin.

Children out on an afternoon walk somehow looked familiar to the Old Tramp. They reminded him of St. Paul, the Sunflower, the Butterfly, the Crow, the Sparrow and the Dove. But this time they were all dressed in everyday, ordinary children's clothes. They were now playing just the roles of children rambling and exploring in the woods. When they saw the Tramp they greeted him.

The Tramp replied, "Well, thank you . . ." He pointed to the various children. "Aren't you St. Paul and aren't you the Sunflower . . and you and you, aren't you the birds who spoke to me a little while ago. The Crow, the Dove, the Sparrow. Well no . . I guess not . . but I do seem to recognize you."

The Tramp fussed around and invited the children to sit on a grassy knoll while birds sang round about them. Then they waited expectantly to hear him tell a story as breezes blew around them and bees hummed.

THE PLAYSCRIPT

OUTLINE OF THE PLAY

SCENE ONE: Easter Morning in the Woods
SCENE TWO: Easter and the Spring
SCENE THREE: The Messenger's Farewell
SCENE FOUR: The Old Tramp and his Friends

An old tramp, traveling in the woods on Easter morning, has a vision of St. Paul. Paul tells how he met Jesus and explains the basis of his good news with the help of visits from such symbolic persons as the Sunflower, the Butterfly, the Crow, the Dove, and the Sparrow.

PRODUCTION NOTES

Ages: 3-17
Two Songs: *The Good Lord is my Shepherd and The Flying Song.*
Actors: Two male adults and five children as symbolic persons
Stage Time: Approximately 25-30 minutes

CHARACTERS IN THE PLAY

The actors may be pre-teens but teens may play the two human adult roles (Old Tramp and St. Paul)

Old Tramp:
A poor vagabond wandering in the woods.

St. Paul:
The Apostle who tells the story of the death of Jesus and Jesus rising up to life again.

The Sunflower:
Explains the idea of death and life, i.e., the life cycle of nature, as a pattern to illustrate the death and the life after death of Jesus.

The Butterfly:
Explains the idea of spring following winter and life following death.

An Old Crow, A Sparrow, A Dove
Messengers of the spring, telling the story of the new life. The old crow represents unlikable people, the sparrow represents small people, the dove represents people with a message. (One or more birds may be added as active but non-speaking participants at the discretion of the producer).

SCENE ONE
AN EASTER MORNING IN THE WOODS

Time: Springtime on a Easter morning at dawn, on a far hilltop in the woods. Center stage is a hilltop thick with trees, bushes, flowers and on the backdrop a light blue and red streaked sky with the sun rising over the hills. The greenery may be stylized or naturalistic. It should contain a selection from birds, rabbits, squirrels, hogs, turkey, deer, fox. There is no path or other sign of civilization. Alternatively, this entire scene may be painted on a front drop (curtain or screen). Old tramp and the messenger then would stand on very small hills, e.g., boxes covered by green carpet at front stage).

Enter an Old Tramp *in dungarees, well-worn walking boots, long-sleeved shirt and wide hat. He carries a small bag on the end of a stick slung across his shoulder. He struggles on the hillside and cannot quite reach the top but, rather, sits down under the shade of a large tree about halfway to the top of the hill. He* *sighs. Several birds sing. Bees hum. A light breeze moves the trees.*

OLD TRAMP: Oh, well, the scenery's good enough from here. *(He takes off his hat and fans himself).* I didn't think it would be as hard as this, on an Easter spring morning. I must be getting middle-aged. And here are the birds that make this Easter dawn a joy.

Sounds of birds and wind in the trees as the Old Tramp points his hat here and there to identify sounds.

In all the many seasons that I have walked in these woods this springtime is the most beautiful. A little warm, a little cool breeze, a little greenery but not enough to spoil the view. A little rain now and then but not too many storms. This is the time of little birds and little squirrels and little rabbits but not too many little flies.

He looks intently into the distance as though just thinking of something.

Why I do believe that spring is the littlest time for little critters that there ever was.

Old Tramp sits down and bows his head. Paul appears on the hilltop looking down towards the Old Tramp. He is dressed in eastern robes, sandals, headgear. He has long white hair. Old Tramp looks up, sees the vision and is startled.

OLD TRAMP: Who are you?

PAUL: I am Paul. I am from another time and place. Don't be afraid. I want only to tell you my story.

OLD TRAMP: What story? Why me?

PAUL: I have been living in heaven. Looking down from there, I saw your weary wandering and I just thought that you would like to hear the good news I bring.

Old Tramp nods, in wonder.

PAUL: Once I too was a traveler like you. That's why I want you to hear my story. For one day I came to understand a true vision of nature and how it works together with our minds and spirits to bring us closer to the great creator. For we can see the works and wonders of the great creator, the maker of everything, in all of the hills and streams and woods and flowers and creatures.

My vision first began when I was traveling in Palestine, many centuries ago. There I met a man called Jesus on the road to Damascus. This man had been put to death by the priests and soldiers of his day - the rulers. They said that Jesus had claimed to be the great creator and that this was a lie. Yet the great maker raised Jesus up from the dead and greeted him as his own son.

OLD TRAMP: I must be dreaming. Here you are and you say you're from heaven and you tell me about a man whom you met, after he was put to death. How could you meet someone who was dead? Was it a ghost that you met?

PAUL: No, it was not a ghost. Jesus had risen up from the dead. And that's why I want all men to believe in Jesus for with His help, by following Him, other people too can hope to rise up from the dead one day. *(gently)* See, that's why I said that I had good news to give you. It's good news to know that after you die you can rise up and live again, isn't it?

OLD TRAMP: Well, I guess so, if I could believe it but I've never been the believing kind. For me to believe *(he hesitates, stumbling)* that . . dead men rise up . . that the dead live again . . that's a bit too much for me. And as for you, Paul, I don't believe in you either. *(sadly)* It's all a dream. I must have fallen asleep . . I'm just dreaming.

Old Tramp falls back into the position of sleeping and snores lightly. Lights fade fully into darkness, signifying sleep.

Curtain

SCENE TWO
EASTER AND THE SPRING

Scene - the same. The Old Tramp is dozing, half asleep in much the same posture and position as before. There is no sign of St. Paul. Bees hum, birds sing and light winds move in the bushes.

Enter the Sunflower wearing brightly colored robes with large wings on its back and a headdress like leaves of a bright yellow sunflower. The dark brown center of the sunflower is located at the front of the headdress, near the forehead or over the crown of the head.

THE SUNFLOWER: *(addressing the Old Tramp)* I am the flower of the sun, each night I sleep and each morning I awake . . just as the sun goes down each night and rises again each morning. Sleeping and waking, death followed by life . . this is the way of the earth. One day my seed will fall into the earth and die in the winter. Then when the rains of spring come and water the seed it will arise up to life again. Winter and spring, that is the

THE FLYING SONG

VERSE ONE:

d^1 l f f - m f r taw_1 d
I will fly along the song-bird's sky
d r m f s l - taw s d^1
Swooping around, a jovial flyer
d^1 d^1 l f f - m f r taw_1 d
To all I know below, I'll call goodbye.
d r m f - l r s m f
While the small people cling - I will fly.
d f m f s l - taw d^1
I'll smile to see their creeping ways
r^1 d^1 d^1 l f s l - d^1 taw l - s
As I climb and rise and circle up higher
d^1 l f f m f r - taw_1 d
I will swing and sing of winging days
d r - m f l r s m f
While above all things I, I will fly.

VERSE ONE:

I will fly along the song-bird's sky
Swooping around, a jovial flyer
To all I know below, I'll call goodbye.
While the small people cling - I will fly.
I'll smile to see their creeping ways
As I climb and rise and circle up higher
I will swing and sing of winging days
While above all things I, I will fly.

VERSE TWO:
High over clouds and rains I'll fly
Far above the fear and lying
A free-bird strong in song and mirth, I'll cry.
From the sad sigh of earth - I will fly
Up where the air is new and true
Through a glad sky where no-one is pining or dying
I will glide in flight across the blue
But above all things I, I will fly.

OLD TRAMP: Amazing but it's true. Maybe there is something in this idea of living and dying and living again. Maybe this is what that white-haired old man was trying to explain to me. Something about Jesus rising up from the dead and flying away and then us too one day . . if we follow Him. I think I'm beginning to see but who's this? More flyers?

Enter the Crow. (cawing loudly) The crow has lean black wings and is dressed in black robes with white/yellow beak.

Enter the Sparrow (chirping slightly) of small slight build with small wings **and a Dove** dressed in white with wide white wings. *(the dove coos gently)*

THE CROW: *(flapping around and crouching down and rising up groaning and creaking).*

Caw . . Caw . . I am the crow. I carry the good news of spring all over the forest. Everybody tries to scare away the crow. They think that I am a bad bird who steals away their seed but I'm not as bad as they think and there is a place for me too in the spring. I too can play my part in making this a lovely springtime. I too rise up and fly and fly and fly. *(runs around stage, flapping wings and cawing like a crow)* Caw . . Caw . . Caw . . .

THE SPARROW: *(jumping around, chirping lightly and shaking its small wings)* Chirp . . Chirp . . . Some people think that I'm too small to be important but that's not true. Small creatures play a big part in making springtime a success. Newts and frogs and tadpoles and flies and bees, also.

THE CROW: And wasps too . . .

THE SPARROW: Yes, you would say that but *(reconsidering)* yes and wasps too and all the little birds. We all fly around and play a big part in the spring.

THE DOVE: I am the Dove. I am the bird with a message for all the world and all people . . good or bad or large or small. I fly out and away and bring the message of peace to everyone but especially in the spring.

THE CROW, DOVE, SPARROW, TOGETHER: We are the messengers of the spring and the new life to boys and girls and men and women all over the world.

THE SPARROW: To great and small.

THE DOVE: To all nations of goodwill.

THE CROW: To the beaten, the harried, the hunted of all times and places. To all who are not well liked, I bring my message too.

ALL THREE: Together, we bring the message of the good news of the spring. Out we go with our good words and fly and fly and fly. *(they move away from the Old Tramp)*

OLD TRAMP: Goodbye, you've helped me to understand things that were not clear to me this Easter morning.
(as the three birds flap their wings and leave the stage, left)

Curtain

SCENE THREE
THE MESSENGER'S FAREWELL

An Easter morning in the hills - the same as Scene One but a little later. The sun may now be a little higher. Old Tramp is sleeping on the hillside, his wide hat pulled over his face. Paul stands at the crest of the hill, looking down at the Old Tramp.

PAUL: Jesus said: "I am the door, by me if any man enter in he shall be saved." Goodbye, Old Tramp. Remember my story and each Easter morning remember to

come to this hillside to enjoy the spring
and to remember . . the story of Jesus.

*Paul throws a small silver coin to
nearby where the Old Tramp is
sleeping. Paul leaves the stage, left,
suddenly, as one disappearing into the
thin air. The Old Tramp is slightly
aroused by the fall of the coin. He stirs,
stretches and awakens. He removes his
hat from his eyes and holds it. He
stands up. He is mystified and
scratches his head with the hand
holding the hat.*

OLD TRAMP: I must have been
dreaming. It must have been a story I
learnt in childhood somehow come back to
me. What would an oldtime Roman
messenger be doing here in these wooded
hills? Oh well, at least it reminds me it is
Eastertime.
    He hesitates, peering at the ground.
What is that gleaming in the sun?
    He picks up a small white coin.
An old, old coin. What is it doing here?
Why, I do believe it's an old penny with an

old tough looking head on it. A head with a wreath of flowers around it. Surely it can't be an old Roman penny? Yet, I think it is. And it's real.

He looks into the distance wistfully.
Yes, I remember the old message. "Render unto Caesar the things that are Caesar's and unto God the things that are God's." Look to the earth as a pattern of life and then look to God to give us a spring . . a new life after death to those who follow Jesus. What a good sermon for Easter. And, funny thing, I didn't even have to go to church. It's all here in the woods. The trees are a chapter. The birds are words. The flies and bees are the commas and dots. The skies are the pages. I can read it all in God's great book of creation.

He brightens.
It's real! It's real! It's a real Roman penny.
(he holds up the coin and jumps for joy)
Yes, it's the real thing. It's real.

Curtain

SCENE FOUR
THE OLD TRAMP AND HIS FRIENDS

Scene - the same. *The Old Tramp is sitting up, going over the Easter story in his head, nodding to himself and muttering and looking at his Roman coin. He stands up.*

OLD TRAMP: Why it's the afternoon already. Soon people will be coming by for walks. I'd better spruce up. *(he straightens up his old clothes)* Then the figure of St. Paul said . . and the Butterfly made a good point . . and the Sunflower explained it so well . . yes, it's good news for all.

Enter the Children on an afternoon walk. They had previously acted the parts of St. Paul, the Sunflower, the Butterfly, the Crow, the Sparrow and the Dove. This time they are all dressed in everyday, ordinary children's clothes. They are now playing the parts of children rambling and exploring in the woods but there should be something in each of their behaviors that reminds the audience of the part they played earlier. For example, the child who acted St. Paul directs the others or remains quiet. The child who portrayed the Sunflower lifts his or her arms to the sun and the former Butterfly flaps her arms around and runs about. The other children run around here and there like birds. When they see the Old Tramp they greet him.

1st CHILD (PAUL): Hey, there's our old friend the tramp.

2nd CHILD (SUNFLOWER): Yes, Old Tramp a happy Easter to you.

OLD TRAMP: Well . . thank you . . *(but pointing to the various children)* . . aren't you St. Paul and aren't you the Sunflower . . and you and you, aren't you the birds who spoke to me a little while ago. The Crow, the Dove, the Sparrow. Well no . . I guess not . . but I do seem to recognize you.

3rd CHILD (SPARROW): Of course you do. We've met before. We're old friends remember, Mr. Tramp?

OLD TRAMP: Yes *(thinking and smiling slowly)* Of course, I remember . . so you're not the Sparrow . . and you're not the Sunflower . . .

4th CHILD (BUTTERFLY): *(excitedly)* Is this a new game Mr. Old Tramp?

OLD TRAMP: No, it's not a game at all but it's an Easter tale worth telling. Yessir. Sit down all of you, sit down right there. *(he points)* Over there on that grassy knoll . . that little green hill.

The Old Tramp fusses around while the birds sing and the children sit on the grassy knoll and wait expectantly. Breezes blow around them and bees hum.

OLD TRAMP: *(slowly)* It seemed to me that you told me a story but that can't be right because you weren't even here then.

No, that could not be so and yet the greatest story of all came to me . . . Let me see now, oh yes, this must be the way of it. Paul passed on a message for all of us. That's it . . . I want to tell you a story . . .

The children smile at each other, sit down quietly and wait expectantly as . . they all sing

THE GOOD LORD IS MY SHEPHERD.

f s   l - l   f   d   taw₁ l₁
The Good Lord is our shepherd
taw₁ d   f   f - f   f
He meets us in our need
s   l   s l   taw   d¹   d¹   l
He leads us by the streams of peace
d¹ taw   r   m   r   d
To fields where we may feed
l   d¹   l   d¹ - d¹   taw - taw l
He brings the spring-time greenness
l   f - f   r - r   taw
We sow the new-life seed
f   s   l - l f d - taw₁
Oh the Lord is still alive
l₁   taw₁ d   f
And He leads us

ALL:
The Good Lord is our shepherd
He meets us in our need
He leads us by the streams of peace
To fields where we may feed
He brings the springtime greenness
We sow the new-life seed
Oh the Lord is still alive
And He leads us

<u>Curtain</u>
END OF PLAYSCRIPT

The Easter Cat

ABOUT THE STORY

Rex McCallister, a mechanical engineer, was about to retire. He and his wife Freiderica had recently moved into a small but pleasant home in an area full of active retirees.

It was springtime and the wind blew leaves around the garden. Freida slept peacefully for two or three minutes then her sleep became unsettled. Suddenly she shook in horror and half-awoke. She stood up quite frightened and stared into the garden.

Freida told Rex about the bad dream she had just had about a wild looking cat that jumped out in front of her and made her heart skip a beat.

Her husband had to leave on his final business trip. Freida walked Rex to the car and kissed him goodbye.

Later in the day there came a gentle knock on the door. Freida opened the door to a policewoman who stood there, hands behind her back and a little nervous. There was a long horrified silence then she spoke quietly, "There has been an accident involving Mr. Rex McCallister."

Freida asked if she could go and see him.

The policewoman shook her head, "There's no need to, not now."

Rex had been killed in a car accident.

The officer whispered, "No one else was involved. An old black cat ran out in front of his car. He braked suddenly but with all the recent rain he just skidded and went off the road. Unfortunately there is quite a drop there. The cat ran off."

About two weeks later, it was Eastertime. Freida was sitting in the patio, reading quietly but stopped suddenly when there was a loud knock on the front door. She opened the door to reveal a figure wearing an Easter Bunny outfit holding a parcel. He presented the parcel to Freida who hesitated and did not yet accept the gift. The Bunny handed over the gift as he read from a card, "Treeridge Farms wishes you a pleasant Easter. We specialize in delivering gifts at the right time. This is for your retirement years from your loving husband Rex."

Freida put the gift on a table. The deliveryman said the present was ordered two weeks ago, then he left. She stared at the gift in amazement. Suddenly she was startled. "I can't believe it. It's alive. It can't be alive. I must be losing my mind."

She tore open the package and was stunned as she lifted out a small kitten. Freida placed the kitten on the table and stroked it with wonder - still surprised at the gift from the beyond. She glanced at the note that was packed with the kitten and read to herself silently and briefly.

The figure of Rex seemed to appear, as a ghost, in the garden. He watched as Freida read out the contents of the note. For a moment Rex seemed to speak. Freida read silently from the note and thought she heard the ghost of Rex speaking. "I know that we will be separated at Easter for the first time in many years but it will only be for a little while. From now on we will not be bound by others, we'll be able to keep pets, so I'm having this little one sent to you. The farm owners will put the pussy in a nice presentation box on Easter Sunday as a surprise."

Freida looked up from reading the note and touched the kitten, stroked it again, gathered it up in her arms and smiled through her tears.

She continued reading the note, "I know that you had a bad dream about cats but I also know that, at heart, you really <u>love</u> cats and all good creatures. Never mind the bad dreams and the bad things that happen in this life. My retirement is just ahead so just look after this little one now and soon we'll be together again for a long time."

She murmured quietly, "A companion and not a stranger - a small friend, a greeting from Rex. A greeting from the other side. A present from our past life - a little Easter Cat."

THE PLAYSCRIPT

OUTLINE OF PLAY

SCENE ONE: Cats Are Dangerous Because . . .
SCENE TWO: Black Cats Are Unlucky And . . .
SCENE THREE: All Cats Are Strangers

PRODUCTION NOTES

Time period - a few weeks. All the action takes place in one set that presents from extreme left stage to extreme right and from front stage to backdrop Freiderica's new home, that is - the garden, the conservatory or glass house, the sitting patio under a solid roof, a short hall area leading to front door and front area.

Although all four main characters in this play are of a mature, coming up to retirement age, both couples (the McCallisters and the Bradys) are fit and healthy, meaning that actors of all mature adult ages might well be able to act the four main parts with suitable makeup, costume and posture and deportment. The other two parts are minor and may be of any age above late teens.

Actors: Three male, three female and one kitten.

Stage Time: About 45 minutes.

Music: One Song: *See You on the Other Side of BigRiver.* This tune may also be used as background music throughout the play.

Set: One large set with four main subdivisions.

Age Group: All

CHARACTERS IN THE PLAY

EASTER BUNNY RABBIT:

A deliveryman

REX MCCALLISTER:

Husband of Freiderica - a mechanical engineer, a big success, who is making his last round before retiring at year's end. Likes pets but has led an unsettled life.

FREIDERICA MCCALLISTER:

Wife of Rex - housewife looking forward to a more settled way of life with less traveling when Rex retires. She dislikes cats.

SOPHISTA BRADY:

A neighbor who also dislikes cats.

MARSHALL BRADY:

A neighbor who likes dogs.

OFFICER COLTRANE:

A policewoman.

SCENE ONE
CATS ARE DANGEROUS BECAUSE . . .

The scene is set in a conservatory, patio and garden filled with rare plants, herbs, leafy trees, flowers and elegant bushes. Many of these delicate and elaborate plants have huge multi-colored tropical leaves and fruits. Some are outdoors, some are shaded by the glasshouse walls and ceiling and some are under the roof of the patio and small hallway.

The front or audience view is that of a cross-section of these exotic areas of the house. There is a door right leading from the small hallway to the front entrance right.

As the curtain rises, Freiderica casually dressed, is discovered sitting on a single wicker armchair, leaning back against the headrest and sleeping peacefully.

Rex and Freiderica (or Freida) McCallister have recently moved into a small retirement home, next door to their old friends Sophista and Marshall Brady.

The gardens are well laid out, lush and thick with herbs, bushes, plants, flowers and the shrubbery extends into the home in the form of pot plants.

The set is divided into four sections, extending the full length and breadth of the stage. Left section one - the back garden of the McCallister home; center left section two - the conservatory with glass roof and walls, wicker chairs and tables; section three center right - the patio or back porch, also filled with shrubbery in pots and boxes, with wooden walls and roof; and section four-right a narrow hallway also with pot plants leading to a main door (or side delivery door) which forms part of the right wall of the set. This door leads to the front or side garden. It needs to be operable for both closing and opening, but glimpses of the front or side garden may or may not be visible to the audience.

As the curtain rises Freiderica, a mature lady semi-formally dressed, is leaning back, sleeping, in a large wicker garden chair, in the conservatory, facing left stage towards the open garden. She is alone on stage, sleeping. She sleeps peacefully for two or three seconds then her sleep begins to become unsettled. She shakes in horror and half-awakens. Then she opens her eyes wide and startled, gasps for breath, holds the arms of her chair, gasps again and then fully awakens. She stands up startled and stares at the garden left.

FREIDA: Get out! Go away! How dare you attack me. *(she blinks seeing nothing)* Where have you gone? *(peering across all the shrubbery of the garden, left)* Oh dear, it must have been a dream - just a nightmare. What a vicious cat!

Enter Rex, Freiderica's husband, *from the inner recesses of their home, right stage. He is mature, about 70'ish and dressed in casual slacks, sports shirt and joggers.*

REX: Did you call out, Freida, are you alright?

FREIDA: I'm all right Rex. I just had a

bad dream about a nasty black cat. It was so brazen. It walked right up to me. It bared its teeth and hissed. It seemed so real. Oh Rex it gave me quite a shock. *(Freida folds her hands across her neck and shudders)*

REX: *(putting his arm across Freida's shoulders)* There. There's a good girl. Don't worry. I often get nightmares when I sleep during the day.

FREIDA: But I was so scared. I thought I was going to die.

REX: But you're not afraid of cats. Remember we used to have a pet cat when we were first married, before we started traveling the world. Remember?

FREIDA: Oh no I've changed my mind about cats. They're evil.

*Enter **Marshall Brady and his wife Sophista (Sophie)**. They are also mature aged, 70'ish or more and dressed casually. They are fit and* *healthy looking, like their friends - the McCallisters.*

REX: Welcome. Sit down. Freida has just had a bad dream about a nasty cat.

Marshall and Sophie sit, relaxed and cheerful.

SOPHIE: Oh, Freida, don't talk to me about cats. We've lived next door here for ten years. Since you've just moved here you probably didn't know it but the neighborhood is coming down with horrible cats. The problem is *(quietly whispering as though in fear of being overheard and pointing to neighbors left and right)* some people take the law literally. Local laws say that dogs should be leashed or under direct control but say nothing about cats. So dogs are leashed or fenced in but cats are allowed to run wild. After you've been here a while you'll mend the old fencing or put in electronic signals that keep out most cats most of the time - you'll find a way to keep them under control.

REX: Now that we're going to be retired, maybe a pet of our own could be trained to help.

MARSHALL: Right, Rex. You mean like a dog, a mean, vicious cat-hating dog. I know one. I can get him for you for free. Just say the word - anytime. My cousin Bob . . .

FREIDA: *(breaking in)* Oh no. I don't think I could cope with a real mean dog just at the present. We've just moved in and . . .

SOPHIE: Of course not. We understand. Marshall means anytime, just when you're ready. I don't much care for dogs that's why we have none but I've always believed that to dream of a cat is a bad omen. I totally hate cats. Black cats are witches in disguise but all cats are dangerous because they know too much and can change from one shape to another to attack children and old people, or so the old superstitions say, and besides, cats are such cold and unfriendly critters.

What's wrong with humans for friends - why is everyone grabbing after animals - dogs, cats, rabbits, gerbils, little white mice - what's wrong with our own fellow human beings?

MARSHALL: I could answer that question but I won't - at least not now, but I've told you so many times before - dogs are faithful, honest and devoted, so why should we look for other pets and companions.

REX: Well, I kind of like dogs. You know my work has kept me and Freida traveling a lot but now that I'm about to retire shortly I feel sure I can find the time to keep a dog or two.

SOPHIE: You know I've had a great idea .

REX: Yes?

SOPHIE: Well when you do retire at the end of the Easter break - why would clients not come here to get help from you rather than you go to them.

REX: *(laughing easily)* Well sure. I'd be only too glad to advise them and give them a plan for say pre-maintenance of their gear all the specifications and timing. But you know - there's not going to be much of that. Most of my work needs for me to be there on the spot. Nobody is going to bring forklifts, hoists, cranes, earthmovers, elevators here to me.

FREIDA: *(nodding cheerfully)* Yes that's why we've had to travel so much all our lives. I didn't mind at first moving house all the time but you know when you move house a whole lot - it seems like you have no home. I'm sick of moving. This place right next door to our old friends - this is going to be a great chance to work this garden and all this shrubbery. I get such a thrill from seeing things grow - plants, animals, children.

SOPHIE: *(looking out over the outer garden, left)* Well, in that case you'll not be so pleased to know that a certain neighbor's cat is ripping up your shrubbery.

A real cat may or may not play a part in the following incident.

FREIDA: *(jumping up and shouting)* Oh no. Where is it? I can't see it.

SOPHIE: *(pointing)* Right there.

REX: *(looking)* Yes, I see something small there, but is it a cat or a dog?

MARSHALL: *(peering)* It's a dog.

SOPHIE: It's a cat. See how it freezes and stares at us. Dogs just run away and they bark.

FREIDA: *(standing up)* Yes I can see it now. It's crouched down, staring at us. It's real guilty looking. It's been digging up our plants, eating them and now it leers and bares its teeth and hisses at us as though we were to blame and not itself. Oh it's just like the cat in my dream. It's horrible. But it's not just me seeing it in a dream. You can all see it.

MARSHALL: Oh it's that old three-legged thing that prowls around. It's just a scaredy cat. The way it hobbles off I call it Hopalong Pussycat.

SOPHIE: *(dashing towards garden left)* Get out, you fiend, you witch. *(stamps her foot)* Shoo. . . Shoo. . . Scat, bad cat *(relaxes)* see its gone to ground into the shrubbery *(looking back at others and sitting down)* Now that was a real bad cat.

Marshall shrugs impartially. Freida sits down quietly.

FREIDA: Oh it's gone - that was all I needed. First I have a nightmare about a mean cat. Then the dream comes true. What is going to be next? What, a cat for Easter - a mischievous, naughty brat. Bad cats are really bad at Easter - an Eastertime cat ought to be good during the season of new life and the spring.

MARSHALL: Well, that's it gone now anyway. Let's just forget it.

REX: I didn't even see it for all the herbs and plants. It must have been a small enough critter. *(looking at his wife)* Just like the small cat we used to have before we started traveling. Remember? Well, I remember him, that wasn't him out there.

SOPHIE: That out there was another bad omen of evil days ahead. Sorry but that's it.

MARSHALL: Listen. I have an idea. Let's talk about dogs.

FREIDA: Oh, of course, I remember how years and years ago my poor old dog ran off somewhere and never came back. Twenty five years ago, it goes out casually as if to check the front gate. Out it meanders like a stranger into the night oblivious of the warm fire and good food and fine couch we had allocated to it.

Yes *(dreamily)* my poor old dog runs off somewhere and never comes back. That's dogs for you. He got in fights, then left us as I suppose he heard beguiling whistles of dog paradise and for all I know he's still riding the doggie hobo trains to the happy hunting places where the bad dogs go.

All remain on stage.

<u>Curtain</u>

SCENE TWO
BLACK CATS ARE UNLUCKY AND . . .

The scene is the same. The stage is now empty.

Enter Sophista, Marshall and Freiderica *from left, as through the garden. They stroll casually in relaxed conversation through the garden and glasshouse until they reach the patio where they sit casually. How long this routine will take, clearly depends on the size of the stage but in all cases the three actors should be seated and pleasantly relaxed at the point where the police officer knocks and enters later, at which point the mood changes to one of shock and horror.*

FREIDA: *(pleasantly)* It is almost Easter. Rex is really looking forward to his retirement. Jobs, he says, are like moulds that you must pour yourself into to survive but you survive as someone else *(looks at watch)* he should be half-way to the airport by now.

SOPHIE: But won't he miss his work after forty years.

FREIDA: He'll miss the work, the technical interest, but not the job, not the boss. They say there's no such thing as a good job. I've worked as a secretary on some of Rex's transfers here and there. And Rex has been continually moved from one project to another. He's a good engineer. We're both glad that we can settle down here and relax. I often wish we'd had our own business. You get sick of trying to please an employer - no matter how hard you try it's never enough.

MARSHALL: *(cheerfully)* Well, I tried working for myself, and believe me you have dozens of bosses to please - they're called creditors and customers.

FREIDA: *(philosophically and shrugging)* Oh them. You pay them or give them good value and they're more than happy - but real bosses, oh no. Seems like they're always taking subtle offense even when you do a good job of work. Even when the boss is socially polite and in good taste. Somehow, your looks, your grooming, your smell, your clothes, your hairstyle, the things you say - the places you go even, all seem to cause some slight offense, some raised eyebrows at times. You can't please them. If you type well and fast - then its a complaint that you don't use all of your fingers. Being there on time is more important than working hard.

SOPHIE: *(smiling and cheerfully)* Oh I know, I've been thru it all too. Workers who come in on time and do next to nothing all day, why the boss thinks the sun rises and sets of them. *(laughs lightly)* But you come in five minutes late and it doesn't matter if you make up for it a hundred times over - you're still a lazy no good parasite. Bosses, men or women - you can't please them. They're always looking you over to see if there's anything out of place.

They sit in the patio, relaxed and cheerful.

FREIDA: *(laughing and holding up her hands like a begging dog)* Right. They treat you like a pup, sitting up doing tricks for your supper and just at the almighty owner's whim or fancy - bang you're fired. The pup is thrown out on the highway - it wasn't clever enough or winning enough - it didn't beg for its supper prettily enough.

SOPHIE: *(casually and looking closely at some plants)* I think its worse for women, you know?

MARSHALL: *(shaking his head and raising his eyebrows)* Oh I rather think not. Men regard their fellow men as much greater rivals for promotion and prestige and stab each other in the back much more often. In fact, its only for the sake of the pension and retirement and the thought of doing your own thing at the end of a long working day and working life - its only the security that may be gained and the thought of escape from the job that makes it all even tolerable.

FREIDA: *(cheerfully)* Oh, I do so much agree with you, Marshall. Rex has had such a hard life in his jobs. He likes the work but he's hauled over the coals if a machine breaks down in three years instead of the three and a half he predicted . . as if anyone can predict the exact future like that. And now he's so glad to be coming home to stay. We have such plans for this garden. It was quite an investment to buy a ready-made herb and vegetable garden like this.

SOPHIE: O do tell us. *(Marshall nods)*

FREIDA: Well we're going to make it all organic - natural gardening to increase the mineral content of the soil and veggies. We'll put in more herbs, add a lavender tree over there. *(points)* Oh yes and make home fresh juices from some of the vegetables. That combined with more exercise . . *(looks around, thinking)* now let me see . . .

SOPHIE: You'll get plenty of exercise just improving a garden like this - no need to run around the block. *(she smiles)*

MARSHALL: That's for sure.

FREIDA: Oh yes and over there some Rosemary, Aniseed and Peppermint . . .

At this point all three are sitting relaxed in casual chairs in the patio, in a cheerful and optimistic mood. There comes a gentle but clear knock on the door. As the policewoman gives her message, the mood of the three is at first still cheerful, then becomes concerned and puzzled and finally they are shocked and horrified.
Freida rises pleasantly to answer the door.

FREIDA: Please excuse me for a moment.

Still smiling and relaxed, Freida opens the door to Policewoman Coltrane who stands there formally in full uniform, hands behind her back and a little nervous. Smiling amiably, Freida addresses the officer.

FREIDA: Yes officer? Can I help you?

OFFICER: *(smiling formally and stiffly)* Are you Mrs. McCallister?

FREIDA: *(politely)* Yes, indeed. How can I help you?

OFFICER: *(a little awkwardly)* I'd like to speak to you, can I step inside just for a few moments?

FREIDA: *(a little surprised but still amiable)* Why . . . Why. . yes, yes of course. Come in.

Officer Coltrane nods slightly formally to Freida and her two friends and steps inside; removes her peaked cap, which she holds in her hands and points it towards a chair tentatively.

OFFICER: May I . . ?

FREIDA: *(closing the front door)* Of course.

Officer Coltrane sits down, smiles again at the Brady's and holds her hat awkwardly between her hands, evidently for Freida to sit down. Freida, sensing a more serious matter than a routine request, and a little uneasy sits down facing the policewoman and glances at the Bradys.

FREIDA: *(to Officer)* These are my very old friends - the Bradys. *(smiling with forced brightness)* We can all talk together. What . . What exactly is the problem?

OFFICER: Well I'm afraid there's been an accident.

MARSHALL: *(quickly)* Outside? Nearby?

SOPHIE: Oh dear. Oh my goodness. Can we help?

Freida stares at the policewoman a little stiffly and querulously.

OFFICER: *(twirling her cap and softly)* Well no. No one here can really help. You see it involves, I'm afraid it involves Mr. McCallister. Mr. Rex McCallister?

FREIDA: *(nodding in acknowledgement of the name and with concern)* Yes, he's my husband. O let's hurry *(standing up)* let's get to him. *(stunned)* Is he in the hospital?

The Bradys stand up, ready to go.

OFFICER: *(rising to be on the same level as the others)* No, there's no real, immediate reason to hurry to be with him.

FREIDA: *(breathing a sigh of relief and holding her neck)* Oh thank heaven. You mean he's on his way home.

Policewoman Coltrane, still standing stiffly and apologetically, shakes her head and looks miserable. There is a long horrified silence.

OFFICER: *(blinking and swallowing)* No, No. I'm afraid not.

Freida still holding her neck and Sophie and Marshall all stare at the policewoman. Freida slips back into her chair, stunned and petrified, staring ahead of her. Marshall and Sophie instinctively rush to each side of Freida and hold her hands and shoulders as she swoons back into her chair.

MARSHALL: *(to officer, gently)* I can't believe it. Are you saying that Rex has been killed?

Officer Coltrane nods.

MARSHALL: *(shaking his head in disbelief)* In a car wreck?
The officer nods again with head bowed.

OFFICER: *(quietly)* I'm afraid so. *(looking at Freida)* There's no point in saying I'm sorry. *(humbly)* Of course I'm sorry - the whole world is sorry. But I've had deaths in my own family and I know that there's nothing that anyone can say that makes any difference - or helps in any way - at a time like this. If there's anything I can do, perhaps, that might help in a few days time if you need advice with funeral arrangements or help with contacting other relatives or informing others - I'll, I'll do what I can . . .

SOPHIE: *(sobbing)* But how did it happen? Rex was such a good and careful driver. Was anyone else involved?

OFFICER: *(almost in a whisper)* There was no blame attached to Mr. McCallister and no one else was involved. According to eyewitnesses, an old black cat ran out in front of him, he braked quickly - the right thing to do - but with the roads being so wet and muddy he, well, he just skidded and went off the road.

    Unfortunately there was quite a drop . . . The cat was seen running off. It's clear your husband loved animals and didn't want to run over one even at the risk of his own life. Conditions along the 21 were real bad.

Freida turns and buries her head in the back of her chair and sobs.

MARSHALL: *(placing his hand on Freida's shoulder)* Thank heavens we were here with you at this time, Freida.

Sophie is stunned and stares ahead as if in a trance. She takes Freida's hand.

SOPHIE: Your dream, Freida - so that was the meaning of your dream - the bad omen - so that was the black old Easter Cat.

Sophie stands holding Freida's hand. Marshall sits beside Freida still with his arm around her shoulder. The policewoman remains standing, looking at the floor, cap in hand. Tableau.

Curtain

SCENE THREE
ALL CATS ARE STRANGERS

As before with minor variations of props. About two weeks later Freiderica is sitting right stage in the patio section of the set. She is knitting, or reading, quietly and solemnly.

__Enter left, from garden, Marshall and Sophie,__ dressed as for a journey but carrying no bags or traveling gear.

SOPHIE: *(gently)* Hi, Freida, darling. This is your last chance *(smiling coaxingly)* to change your mind and join us for our Easter break.

MARSHALL: *(with concern)* Yes, you know our daughter would be so happy to have you along, as well as us and also *(shaking his head regretfully)* it's so bad to be alone at Eastertime - after such a great loss, such a shock . . .

SOPHIE: Really, Freida, you shouldn't spend Easter alone here with wild cats invading your garden - cats that give you nightmares.

FREIDA: Yes that dream was so vivid and strange.

SOPHIE: I know but all cats are strange. They're just strangers by nature - self-contained and hateful. Do come stay with us.

FREIDA: *(shaking her head quietly but gratefully)* It's so good of both of you to invite me to be with you but I . . I really should be here. Just here. *(thoughtfully)* You know Easter is a time for hope and a new beginning . . .

SOPHIE: *(interrupting with concern)* Oh no. You're family to <u>us</u>. Family and friends are one to us . . .

FREIDA: *(waving away Sophie's interruption)* Oh that wasn't what I meant. I know I'm just like part of your family. What I'm trying to say . . look . . <u>my</u> family <u>somehow</u> is here. I know that

Rex is dead but somehow . . well this was to be our retirement home - somehow I feel his presence here - as though he lingered. Rex lives on.

Looking sadly at the four corners of the ceiling.

It's hard to explain, but it's as though somewhere on some far-off highway of life where past and present and future meet. It is as though some memory of Rex lingers on here. It's like he belongs here even though he's gone. I don't know how to say it but I *(she hesitates sadly)* . .

I just can't bring myself to walk out, to desert his rightful place . . his memory. Maybe he's really here trying to get in touch with me in some way. I do not know, I just have this feeling that I ought to be here and not off somewhere else trying to forget, oh no, I should be here trying to accept all that has happened. I should be here where Rex's memory is. *(plaintively)* Do you know what I mean?

MARSHALL: *(solemnly and decisively)* I do *(he looks at Sophie who nods sadly and Sophie nods in return more brightly)* This is <u>all</u> yours to decide. We'll see you after the holidays. All right?

Freida nods, pleased to have made her point and rises. All three shake hands pleasantly. Sophie kisses Freida goodbye.

SOPHIE: If you change your mind *(points to the phone)* Anytime, O.K? *(raises her hand to her chin, pensively and then points to Freida)* but I think I know what you mean.

FREIDA: *(nodding to the couple)* Thank you.

Sophie and Marshall leave stage left, waving to Freida. Freida sits down and continues reading or knitting or sewing, etc., then pauses and stares into the distance painfully. She meditates for a few moments, then looks strangely around the room.

FREIDA: *(quietly and sadly)* Oh Rex. Where are you? Where have you gone? How can I be here, so alone when you are supposed to be with me until . . oh yes, until death us do part . . . Oh yes, that's it, that's the explanation until death us do part. And this is it. Death.

Freida begins to weep softly and gently but stops suddenly and painfully when there is a loud knock on the front door, right stage.

FREIDA: *(approaching door and placing her ear alongside the lock and bolt)* Who is it?

VOICE: *(cheerful and loud)*   I'm the Easter Bunny.

FREIDA: *(not hearing fully)* Who?

VOICE: *(still cheerful)* The Easter Bunny.

FREIDA: *(hearing and shaking her head)* Don't be ridiculous. Go away. I've no time for tricks.

VOICE: *(still loud but seriously)* Ma'am, I'm sorry. I'm supposed to say that. We're a delivery service. I have an Easter parcel for you. We're Treeridge Farms - we do special deliveries.

FREIDA: *(still suspicious)* Who sent it?

VOICE: *(reading mechanically)* Rex McCallister.

Freida starts slightly in surprise, pauses, hesitates and then opens the door to reveal someone dressed in an Easter Bunny outfit holding a parcel. He presents the parcel to Freida who hesitates and does not yet accept the gift.

FREIDA: *(shaking her head)* But this is impossible.

BUNNY: *(mechanically)* Treeridge Farms wishes you a pleasant Easter. We send out all kinds of specialty gifts at all times of the year, guaranteed delivered just at the right moment for that special time of your life - birthday, anniversary or remembrance moment. . .

The Easter Bunny reads from the parcel.

Happy retirement Mrs. McCallister.
(handing over gift and reading from card)
For your retirement years - a gift from your loving husband Rex.

Freida puts the gift on a table, reaches into a drawer or handbag and hands a gratuity to the Easter Bunny delivery-man.

FREIDA: *(still puzzled)* When was this sent?

BUNNY: *(reading from his card)* About two weeks ago ma'am. But scheduled for delivery today *(smiles brightly)* Easter Day. Thank you ma'am. A happy Easter to you dear lady.

The Easter Bunny deliveryman leaves. Freida closes the front door and stares at the gift in amazement, shaking her head.

FREIDA: *(incredulously)* About two weeks ago, before Rex was killed he sent this gift to me to be delivered on Easter Sunday. *(thinks)* Oh yes. I did ask him to have some Easter Eggs delivered from the farm . . he sent it to arrive today. What a nice idea. *(she shakes her head)* But I couldn't eat anything now on my own. And besides, the deliveryman has damaged the packing. It's ripped open. There are holes in it. *(she examines the parcel and speaks slowly)* But these seem to be real holes . . round and neat and meant to be there.

(Freida looks curiously at the present. Suddenly she is startled. Pauses and listens carefully) I can't believe it. It's alive. It can't be alive. I must be losing my mind.

She tears open the package and is stunned by what she sees. She lifts a sheet of paper out of the box, glances at it and stares into the gift box again. She shakes her head in disbelief, lifting out a small kitten.

Freida places the kitten on the table. It is leashed to the fairly weighty delivery box to prevent it running around.

Freida strokes the kitten in wonder and awe - still surprised at the gift from the beyond. She glances at the letter that was packed with the kitten.

She reads the note to herself silently and briefly. The figure of Rex appears, as a ghost, left stage among the herbs and flowers, reciting the contents of the note. Lighting focuses faintly on Rex as he speaks and then the light dims, fades and goes out as he finishes his short message. Freida reads silently from the note and does not see the ghost of Rex.

REX: I know that we will be separated at Easter for the first time in many years but it will only be for a little while. From now on we will not be bound by others, we'll be able to keep pets, so I'm having this little one sent to you on Easter Sunday.

REX sings

SEE YOU ON THE OTHER SIDE OF BIG RIVER
Sung: Cheerfully and Sentimentally

REFRAIN:

d m - m   m - m m - m - m m   r - d
I'll see you on the other side of BigRiver
d f - f   f   f - m - m   m   m - r
I'll see you when we cross the cruel tide
d m   s - s   m   f - f l   l - l
I'll see you sister and I'll see you, brother
f   m - m   m - m   r - r   d
I'll see you on the other side.

VERSE ONE:

d   r   m   m   m   m   m   r   d   d
Where the deaf shall hear, where the lame shall leap
d   d f - f   f   f m - m m m   r
Where the lonely shall be lively as a bride
d   m   s   s   s   m   f - l   l   l
Where the eyes of the blind shall be opened for ever
d   m   s   s - s   m   f   l l - l
Where sorrow and dying will trouble us never
d m   s   s   s - m   f   l   l   l
I'll see you where the great waters heal us for ever
d m   s   s - m   f   l   l - l
I'll see you on the other side of the river
f m   m   m   r   r - r   d
I'll see you on the other side.

REFRAIN:
I'll see you on the other side of BigRiver
I'll see you when we cross the cruel tide
I'll see you, sister, and I'll see you brother
I'll see you on the other side.

VERSE ONE:
Where the deaf shall hear, where the lame shall leap
Where the lonely shall be lively as a bride
Where the eyes of the blind shall be opened for ever
Where sorrow and dying will trouble us never
I'll see you where the great waters heal us for ever
I'll see you on the other side of the river
I'll see you on the other side.

VERSE TWO:
O, I'll see you where departed ones are living forever
Where the long hills will blossom far and wide
Where everyone tends his own garden of trees
And the wine of the vine is long life and peace
Where the fish are flowing and frisky in the seas
And those who fish will be always at ease
I'll see you on the other side.

I know that you had a bad dream about
cats but I also know that, at heart, you
really <u>love</u> cats and all good creatures.

Never mind the bad dreams and the bad things that happen in this life. My retirement is just ahead so just look after this little one now and soon we'll be together again for a long time.

Freida looks up from reading the note. The lights dim on the ghost of Rex. Freida touches the kitten, strokes it, gathers it up in her arms and smiles through her tears.

FREIDA: A companion and not a stranger - a small friend, a greeting from Rex. A greeting from the other side. An Easter present from our past life - a little Easter Cat.

Curtain
END OF PLAYSCRIPT

Zakotu
the Werewolf

ABOUT THE PLAY

Mysterious murders have been taking place in the remote villages of the great swampland. A savage wolflike but apparently human killer has been seen briefly by terrified witnesses to the crimes. This killer seems to disappear into the air after the murders. Rumors among the fishing people say the werewolf is a master actor who can look like anyone - possibly he is an ancient one returned to take revenge on the newcomers who have ravaged the land - they call him Zakotu, the Spirit of the Swamps.

The play begins when Matilde, the mother of the local priest, is about to usher in an old friend. The friend is Doloree, a nun and nurse. Or is she? Indeed, is anyone what they are supposed to be? Matilde is murdered. So, whodunit?

Who is taking control in the remote villages among the great swamps? The whole series of mysterious killings revolves around the presbytery, parish church and graveyard. Poor frightened swampland dwellers call for investigations from the outside world. The leading investigator is Felix O'Neill, the master detective of all time and all places, who develops a strange and unusual theory of werewolfism. Does this theory explain the sinister murders? If so, who or what is the werewolf? There are twelve likely suspects. The main dramatic impact comes from Felix O'Neill's brilliant investigation, the eerie disguises of the werewolf and the scary events, set in the misty swamps.

OUTLINE OF THE PLAY

Play based on
the novel - Werewolf Murders

ACT I - THE WEREWOLF WALKS
Scene One: An Old Friend Visits
Scene Two: A Touch of History

ACT II - WHO IS THE WEREWOLF?
Scene One: The Werewolf Analyzed
Scene Two: An Eyewitness Talks
Scene Three: Blanche's Testimony Discussed
Scene Four: What is a Werewolf
Scene Five: What the Priest Thinks

ACT III - THE WEREWOLF TRIUMPHS
Scene One: An Eyewitness is Silenced
Scene Two: The Priest's Denial
Scene Three: An Unwelcome Guest Arrives

ACT IV - TRIAL OF A WEREWOLF
Scene One: A Jury of Werewolves
Scene Two: Judgment and Mystery
Scene Three: Hopes Renewed

PRODUCTION SPECIFICATIONS

DURATION: A few days or weeks.
COUNTRY: Anywhere in the world.
SEASON: The spring.
PERIOD: A long time ago.
LOCATION: The play is set in a remote part of a great swampland in and around a large rambling graveyard.
STAGE TIME: Approximately 170-200 minutes.
AGES: Actors and audiences from teens to adult.
ACTORS: Ten men and ten women.

SET: The simplest and most labor-effective method is to have one large divided set for four scenes (five counting the up stage walkway between the curtain and the flood-lights) as follows:

	1. Crypt Church Open Open	
2. Old Abbey Hall and Library Open	3. Graveyard Open	4. Priest's House Open
	APRON ~ Upstage	

1. Downstage, left to right, a crypt set lower than the sanctuary with a step or two leading down to the crypt, pews and organ with props or painted scenery representing pews and organ, perhaps altar or pulpit extreme right, open to upstage (audience).

2. Leftstage, a window extreme left through which can be seen three hanging nooses. The window is surrounded by extensive bookshelves, with large reading tables and chairs set around. This subset is open to upstage (i.e., audience) and right to centerstage (i.e., graveyard).

3. Centerstage. Open to upstage and the audience - the graveyard furnished with traditional Christian symbols, such as, but not limited to, angels, tombstones, crosses, kerbs, urns, herbs, statuettes, wreaths and so on. These symbols should not be typical of any <u>one</u> denomination, i.e., Celtic or orthodox or catholic crucifixes, rosaries, etc. The churchyard is dismal and dreary and covered with bushes, trees, ivy, flowers, shrubbery and undergrowth. Bound on three sides by (1) crypt and church, (2) the Old Abbey left and (4) the priest's house - all open to upstage and the audience.

4. Rightstage, open to centerstage (graveyard) and upstage (audience) is the priest's house furnished with bookshelves, tables, dressers, large chairs, and objects of art. On the downstage "wall" of the house if a barred window and barred heavy door. This door leads downstage and to the center so that there is actor access between this door and the graveyard.

5. The upstage or apron area just in front of the footlights is used in the finale. At the finale, the rest of the set may remain open and uncurtained with dimmed lights or the curtain may be down if there is enough room on the apron. All will depend on the size of the apron. No properties or scenery is needed here (although the valises are carried by the

departing guests).

6. Other Set Methods: Stage instructions in the play assume the above multiple set is used. However, although this multiple stage set will be best for most companies, if good storage and plenty of labor is available the scenes may be changed in between curtain falls and rises. A revolving stage pre-set for each scene would be ideal. For film or video, on location is recommended, in an old church, graveyard, village, manse, rectory or similar historic sites.

The choices are:

1 – Multiple Stage Set in film studio or theatre

2 – Serial Change Sets

3 – Rotational Sets

4 – On location

Any one of these traditional methods may well provide atmosphere for this chilly mystery. More modern and experimental methods may not do so.

CHARACTERS IN THE PLAY

DR. ARTURO GARZON: Healtharian and Homeopath, friend and gentleman-at-arms to Mr. Felix O'Neill. Short, broad-shouldered, stocky, slightly fat – his accent has traces of places he has visited – Scots, Irish, Northcountry, Welsh, Westcountry, American, Canadian, South African and Australian.

MR. FELIX O'NEILL: A former accountant and business law expert with a background in the logical scientific methods of economics. Progressing from investigative auditing, he has now become the world's leading consulting detective. Of medium height, lean, hawk-nosed, ruddy complexion, blue-eyed, brown auburn hair, powerfully strong and fast on his feet. He speaks the Queen's English with no trace of an Irish, or other, accent.

SERGEANT ANTOINE: Chief Constable.

MADAME LA PROFESSEUR, VERMILLION LAFLEURE: A forensic scientist also called upon by the locals to help solve the murders.

ANNE: Hostess of the Inn.

THE ABBESS MOTHER CONCORDEE: The Mother Superior of the Old Abbey and Convent.

SISTER PAPILLION AND SISTER PRUDENCE: Sisters, elderly nuns in the Abbey.

PIERRE THE CURATOR: Curator of the Museum of the Inquisitors.

FR. CHARLES: A priest of the parish.

CANON LOUIS: A lawyer of the church.

BLANCHE: A young kitchenmaid at the Inn.

SISTER DOLOREE: An old nun and visiting nurse, from the Abbey.

JANICE: The priest's housekeeper.

ELENE: Janice's daughter and a church servant.

MICHEL: Blanche's boyfriend.

MATILDE CHARLES: Mother of the priest.

ZAKOTU: The werewolf.

TWO OR MORE GUARDSMEN OR POLICEMEN.

EXTRAS: Occasional servants, villagers and travelers are optional extras.

SCENE: The great misty swamplands where old traditions, old nobles, ancient church dignitaries, still rule the parish.

ACT ONE
The Werewolf Walks

Scene One:
An Old Friend Visits

Scene One is Subset 4 - The Priest's House (see chart). The stage set is designed as a horseshoe open to the audience. Along the back is the church with pews, small crypt to the left, a few steps up from the crypt, the sanctuary to right center is all open with framed doors and windows. Right stage the priest's house and left stage the Abbey also open to audience.

Time: *Early evening, after dark.*

Center Stage: *are tombstones, graves and statuettes of saints, angels, the Virgin or crosses. The graveyard is shadowy and sinister and encroaches almost on the house, covering paths and walls with tropical flowers and plants, ivy and overhanging weeping willow, cypress trees heavy with Spanish moss. Birds call and hoot grotesquely in the mangroves.*

Right Stage: *is the interior of the priest's parlor library, the wall of the house dividing the stage in two from back to front. There is no door in this wall, perhaps a window or two depending on the size of the stage. This wall meets the front wall of the house at back stage,* *forming a rectangular room. The front wall of the house stretches from the side wall to right center stage and is therefore in full view of the audience. The audience look in thro the back of the priest's house.*

Set in this front (of the house) wall is a window, and a door, at least one half of which is glass, leading to the outside of the house, back right. This area can be seen by the audience, as being strewn with whinbushes and trees, through the glass door or through the window beside the door.

Both door and window are securely barred. Thus, the window and door fully flat face the audience, giving the impression of looking out through the door into the darkened garden beyond, immediately adjacent to the graveyard.

The door and window should be large, and although fairly downstage, clearly visible to the audience, and covered with clear glass so that callers and visitors as they wait outside the priest's house, can be seen by the audience. The back wall of the parlor is open to the audience.

The inside of the parlor - a kind of lounge-library is furnished with large tables, chairs, bookcases, pillars in the mid room area, a small organ near the right wall, if space permits, perhaps dressers/cabinets. Furnishings are lavish, large pot plants, carpets, cushions, portraits, curtains at door and windows.

Zakotu the Werewolf

The audience is looking into the priest's large parlor where guests visit and looking outback through his partly glassed front door. Much of this scene can be presented on painted screens - the rest by props.

The room is lit by candles but it is clear that moonlight plays a part in the lighting of the room. At left backdrop in the background beyond the graveyard's presbytery can be seen the old church, with door, window/roof, the tower, part of the spire.

From the church comes the sound of slow, eerie, traditional church organ music. The view of the house right consists mainly of the internal scene of the library lounge, with just a little of the surrounding brickwork being visible.

The surroundings are mysterious and somber and the impression is created of looking in on the presbytery room at a time when the inhabitants are vulnerable and dominated by the grim rays of the moon above the church and above the churchyard outside, bearing down on the library scene.

In the presbytery, the mother of the local priest has just ushered in and is now talking to an old friend - Doloree, an old nun and visiting nurse. She is thin wizened and quite old and dressed in gray long outdoor robes, white gloves and cowl. Doloree appears edgy and uncomfortable, looking around nervously at times.

Matilde, the Priest's mother, an elderly woman in black dress with white lace was alone in her parlor. She is comfortable and at ease and is pleasant and gracious to her visitor.
During their conversation a maid, Elene, inconspicuously comes and goes, *dusting and arranging among the large furniture of the old fashioned library.*

MATILDE: *(in a gossipy, matter of fact manner)* The question is, who and what is a werewolf? There's no question that there have been more than a few mysterious deaths around here recently. It's only now that it's becoming common knowledge but it's long been believed by some that a werewolf is walking at night.

DOLOREE: You're making me nervous. *(leaning forward inquiringly)* Of course people, especially young people, do tend to leave these remote parts - sometimes just running off without warning their families - so thoughtless and selfish.

MATILDE: I suppose that's true too but there have been terrible murders recently with bodies found torn apart.

DOLOREE: *(continues shocked)* Heaven protect us. I can never quite understand how a werewolf can live among Christians or just what kind of a creature it is. I mean, is it man or beast?

Elene comes and goes inconspicuously.

DOLOREE: *(continuing to be tense and looking around nervously)* Well, as the mother of Fr. Charles, you're certainly in a position to meet with many visitors, as well as all the important people of the parish, so you must get some sort of opinions. As a simple religious and nurse I only meet the poor of the parish.

Doloree smiles slightly, shrugs and shakes her head.

Of course, I have heard a few rumors of killings in the outlying parts - but I took it to be the work of bandits. Dear, dear, as you say, what exactly is a werewolf? *(in a slightly sinister manner)* A kind of man-monster but is there really such a thing?

MATILDE: Fr. Charles is certainly worried about the killings and the presence of a werewolf. He has warned me several times, "Mother," he says, "be careful whom you let into the presbytery. Something in disguise is finding its way into the homes of the people. Something is walking in the jungles and swamps. Be careful," he says, "Please promise me you will, Mother."

Elene enters right stage quietly, unseen by others, does some light dusting and arranging at a bookcase or dresser.

DOLOREE: *(stands up, strangely looking around and listening carefully)* Matilde, we are alone aren't we?

MATILDE: Certainly Doloree, and of course, you may speak to me confidentially at any time if you have any problem. No one else will disturb us.

Doloree sits, smiles awkwardly, with patent insincerity.

DOLOREE: *(hesitantly)* Yes, I'm a little nervous. It's just these mysterious murders we're talking about, mostly of women, have upset me more than I like to admit. I was . . well . . trying to play it down. But I must admit I'm afraid . . my work . . as you know . . yes, my work as a nurse requires me to travel about at all hours of the day and night.

Doloree looks concerned and worried as one bidding for sympathy.

MATILDE: *(with deep sympathy)* Of course, how silly of me not to have thought of that. It must be terrifying for you. Here I am, almost afraid to answer the door and yet I'm safe and protected in the presbytery - for who would dare to enter the house of a priest on an unlawful mission? My son, Fr. Charles, really does worry unnecessarily - and there you are, out in the woods and highways at all hours of the day and night on call to almost anyone.

DOLOREE: *(looking sideways, shiftily)* Matilde, what is this werewolfism anyway?

MATILDE: No one is quite sure. It's nothing for you to worry about. I'm sure that these creatures, whatever they are, man or beast can't harm any true Christian. I'm sure that our Lady always protects all of us especially you religious on your godly visits to those who need you.

DOLOREE: Really, but what do we actually know of the werewolf then, Matilde?

MATILDE: *(with a confidential and informative air)* It's said to be a shapeshifter.

DOLOREE: A what? *(stares at Matilde)*

MATILDE: A creature that changes its shape from man to beast, or beast to man and that's how it comes into the homes of its victims. It can take many different forms - *(stares at Doloree in quizzical contemplation. Doloree looks stunned)* Doloree, are you sure. .?

DOLOREE: *(quickly and suspiciously)* Sure of what?

MATILDE: Are you sure that I'm not frightening you?

Doloree smiles and it's clear that Matilde isn't suspicious of Doloree.

DOLOREE: *(smiling and caressing her hair, in a gesture of relief)* No Matilde, as one who travels a lot . . at night . . I need to know these things.

MATILDE: Of course you do, my dear. That's why I'm mentioning these rumors. *(as one justified in something dubious)* You see . . I'm not trying to panic you, just trying to . . well, inform you . . so that you will be forewarned and forearmed . . .

DOLOREE: *(primly)* Of course, just for my own safety. You're extremely well informed, Matilde. I knew you would be. That's why I came to see you.

MATILDE: *(smiling warmly)* Yes, exactly. Anyway where was I . . ?

DOLOREE: The shapeshifter.

MATILDE: Ah, yes. I think that's just about the latest talk in the parish. *(raises her hand and flicks it towards Doloree in a gesture that says, Of course, I remember now)* Yes indeed.

Matilde raises the index finger of her waving hand to pinpoint the exact theme of her conversation.

That was it . . the fishing folk call him Zakotu. Some say that he's the reincarnation of an Old Spirit of the Indigenos. He's the one who changes and is now here hiding and walking among us.

DOLOREE: *(standing up suddenly)* How could such a creature hide? How could we not see it lurking among the trees or behind the furniture? It's impossible, a werewolf can't just disappear. We'd be bound to see it.

MATILDE: *(shaking her head, gently)* No, you don't understand *(intently)* Doloree, it takes on different forms so that we don't recognize it.

Elene leaves quietly but makes a slight noise in the course of her chores. As Elene leaves, Matilde hears the noise, stands, looks behind her puzzled.

MATILDE: Did I hear a noise just then? Surely we're alone? It must have been Elene?

Doloree stands up and subtly and inconspicuously flexes her fingers, claw-like at Matilde. However, Doloree quickly sits down as Matilde turns her attention back to Doloree.

DOLOREE: These things are mysteries.

MATILDE: *(aside)* I thought I smelled garlic. Surely no one has been cooking at this time of the evening? Still, the servants sometimes do their own thing.

(in response to Doloree) Yes, mysteries, as you say, Doloree. Of course, one can speculate but no one knows for sure. It's all part of the great mystery of the undead - the returners who live beyond the bounds of humanity.

DOLOREE: To kill others?

MATILDE: *(with some fear)* Apparently. That's why it's good to know that maybe these mysteries will soon be solved by the scholars of good and evil who have come here to study all the murder and mutilation.

DOLOREE: *(interested)* Who and where?

MATILDE: At the Inn there's a young lady professor of forensic science who has been sent for to investigate the murder. She's been looking up tales of horror and has already written a book about some kind of a monster. The famous detective Felix O'Neill and his assistant Dr. Garzon have also been sent for. Isn't it marvelous to think that all these experts are here to solve these murders and to help us find the killer? Our little village is becoming quite infamous.

DOLOREE: No wonder, Matilde.

Enter Elene, returning on another routine task, quietly, unseen by others. Doloree now stands fairly close to Matilde and behind her leaning over her.

MATILDE: Doloree, that's funny. I seem to smell garlic again. Anyway, I see that you're anxious about these things. *(in a kindly way)* I'm only an old lady but my son, Fr. Charles, has a book about magic and werewolves. It was written by a saintly author for our protection. Would you like to read it? I'm sure it would be alright if I lent it to you.

DOLOREE: Thank you so much, Matilde. I would like to read it very much.

MATILDE: Well then, let me get the book for you.

Matilde gets up, quite oblivious of any danger and goes to the nearest bookshelf, begins to scan the titles with her back to Doloree.

MATILDE: Let me see . . .

Doloree assumes a posture of slight aggressiveness, hands clawed and teeth bared just a little and then relaxes as Matilde turns around.

MATILDE: Please be seated, Doloree. Do relax.

Doloree sits briefly, then, as Matilde turns back to the bookshelf rises again.

I'm sure there's no one to overhear us. Don't be nervous.

Elene doesn't hear the conversation and continues her dusting and arranging quietly as Matilde continues to look for the book. Doloree draws close to Matilde and resumes her former hand - claw ready to strike posture, with greater ferocity than before and in complete silence. She does not approach Matilde at first.

MATILDE: *(crying out in enthusiasm)* Ah . . here it is. . this is it.

As attention is focused on Matilde and her book-find, the moonlight is obscured by a cloud, lights fade as Doloree turns into a werewolf. Any successful technique may be used to achieve this transformation. For instance, by Doloree turning away and removing the facemask, gloves and wig of an elderly nun, revealing the werewolf underneath or by means of a substitute actor as Doloree steps behind a pillar or bookcase and a werewolf steps into her place, wearing similar clothes. Werewolf strikes at Matilde from behind. Matilde turns around with book in hand and screams horribly in unbelief, drops book as werewolf comes closer and seizes her by the throat.

MATILDE: *(screams loudly in horror)* The wolf's got my throat - help.

Matilde falls behind a chair, which hides the carnage, as the werewolf begins to tear Matilde apart. Matilde's screams are joined by the screams of Elene. The werewolf pauses, looks *around as for another victim, but hides behind a pillar or piece of furniture and becomes silent.* **The werewolf** *listens and, hearing others approaching,* **leaves by way of the front door** *and disappears among the graves.* **It exits the stage from the graveyard to the left.***

After a significant pause **enter from right Fr. Charles, the priest** *in full frock, apparently shocked and frightened and tearful.*

Enter Elene's mother Janice, *the housekeeper, an old lady dressed in long black gowns. They rush to the scene of the murder and look down at the body in horror. Fr. Charles prays briefly in silence.* **Elene emerges from hiding, weeping.**

ELENE: Mother, it was a werewolf. One moment Fr. Charles' mother was speaking to Sister Doloree the nurse and then all of a sudden a werewolf seized dear old Matilde. Oh, dear heavens . . it was horrible!

FR. CHARLES: But where's Sister Doloree? What's happened to her?

ELENE: I don't know, Fr. Charles. She just seemed to disappear. The moon went down behind the clouds, I think. The candles aren't strong.

JANICE: Was Sister Doloree taken away by the werewolf then?

ELENE: Maybe. I don't know. I wasn't watching closely. I was hiding then listening in the silence after Matilde was killed.

FR. CHARLES: Think carefully, Elene. This is important. Was Doloree and the werewolf here at the same time or did Doloree run off when the werewolf arrived?

ELENE: *(in tears)* Fr. Charles, I don't know. There was a horrible silence when I thought that the werewolf was listening to hear me breathing, so as to kill me. I heard a sound like a swish of skirts as it fled. I'm sorry, I just don't know.

The women weep.

Fr. Charles walks away from the immediate murder scene to center of room, stares as in a state of shock.

FR. CHARLES: *(looking at the audience)* I tried so hard to be careful and yet somehow the werewolf was able to <u>walk</u> even into the house of the religious. Who knows, perhaps it was disguised as Doloree *(puts his hand to his eyes to suppress weeping, shakes his head)* and I was just reading the words of the patriarch Job, "Alas, the thing that I greatly feared has come upon me." Something evil is walking in these swamps and jungles - no doubt a werewolf, a destroyer of the flock - but who or what is a werewolf?

CURTAIN

ACT ONE
The Werewolf Walks

Scene Two:
A Touch of History

Scene Two is set in the great hall of the old abbey, left stage, in the multiple set. Around the sides of the hall are shelves filled with large ecclesiastical, legal and scientific heavily-bound books.

Right center and upstage are large tables and chairs. On some of these tables are huge open volumes and piles of closed books as though someone has been studying or browsing. Some pens and ink and paper are on the tables. Traditional artifacts, artwork and tapestries are on the walls.

The left wall of the stage is a screen and contains pictures of the nearby museum of "confessions" where at one time suspects and witnesses were interrogated and intimidated prior to the trials that took place in the religious courts of orthodoxy many years ago. There are pictures of medieval torture, the screw, the claw, the rack, the Iron Maiden, the spider.

There is a large barred window also forming part of the left wall of the chamber and three (empty at present) hangmen's nooses can be seen hanging in the yard outside. The simplest way to present this is to have a painted paper poster of the window and nooses - to be replaced later by a poster of three persons hanging. As the scene opens left, the library is lit by candlelight. The Abbess is already poring over books at one of the tables. She is an elderly woman of slight build and weight, weak and wizened in figure.

Enter the Canon with Felix O'Neill and Dr. Garzon. O'Neill is lean, muscular, hawkish, dressed in long outdoor leggings, light tweed cloak, walking stick, robinhood hat and strong walking boots. He is followed by a Dr. Garzon, his right-hand man, broad-shouldered and stocky. Garzon sports a walrus moustache, sideburns and is slightly overweight but of a powerful build. He is dressed in brown tweeds. They are ushered in by two nuns. They are more elderly and frail than the Abbess and are dressed in long robes. They retire at once after bowing over the hand of the Abbess.

The Canon is a thin, stiff, mature man. He wears a perpetually worried expression, as *though weighed down by the burdens of law and exegesis, in particular by his chronic inability to believe anyone about anything.*

Canon Louis as a lawyer of the church has also been called upon occasionally by secular authority to act as a magistrate on local minor misdemeanors. These occasional appointments are part-time, minor, and at the discretion of the local mayor, but nonetheless somewhat prestigious appointments as recognizing the Canon's integrity, knowledge of law and status on the local areas. His look of innate concerned skepticism is accentuated by a tendency to shake his head slightly every few seconds, a purely nervous disorder, but one that seemed always to communicate a subtly worried, negative message, as if to say, "No, I am afraid I can't quite accept that. That worries me. There must be some misunderstanding."

One wondered if this involuntary negativism was the result of long years of learnt skepticism in the tombs of justice or whether it was a mere nervous twitch, so suited to an inquisitional scholar, that it was, years ago, shrewdly recognized as a professional asset by his superiors and resulted in his receiving the appointment of Canon of Law in the first place. It is sad to think that a twitch in the neck may be as good as a Masters Degree in Law, but such is life.

CANON: Your highness, my dear Abbess. It is most gracious of you to grant us an audience *(shakes his head - No, No, says the gesture)* you are so deeply concerned about the welfare of your humble religious. You are so devoted to justice. *(No, No, he twitches)* so keen to bring the murderer of the flock to . . .

ABBESS: *(interrupting him, with a casual wave of the hand)* Enough my dear Canon, time enough for a eulogy when I'm dead. *(smiling at Felix O'Neill)* But that I hope will not be for a little while, a few months yet. I am old as you can see. You must be Mr. Felix O'Neill the author of several monographs on criminals in disguise. I hope that we can work together. I am the Abbess Concordee.

O'NEILL: I'm so pleased to meet you Abbess and this gentleman is my friend Dr. Garzon who is here to assist with our investigations.

The Abbess briefly smiles and nods towards Dr. Garzon.

ABBESS: You may be aware that our village's elevation here is just a little above the nearby swamps and jungles. I hope you will find it healthy. I want very much to solve these crimes against the people and I feel sure that we're getting closer to the truth.

Earlier I asked Canon Louis to arrange for the questioning of one of our nuns, Doloree, a nurse who, unfortunately, is our chief suspect at the moment. *(to Louis)* She has gone missing from the Abbey. Did you attend to this, Louis?

CANON: *(twitching negatively)* Yes, your highness. I sent Sergeant Antoine to find her. I understand that she is in hiding - a sure sign of guilt.

O'NEILL: Or fear, or unsociability or desire for peace and quiet or being away visiting as a nurse or away seeking information - I have often been in "hiding" myself for some of these reasons.

CANON: *(with sinister and threatening sharpness)* Guilt and fear of punishment is the most obvious reason. *(twitching No, No)* Mr. O'Neill this chamber, besides being a library, is the higher ecclesiastical and traditional courtroom for this parish. Common crimes such as theft and drunkenness and fraud and fighting are dealt with in the village courtroom. Graver matters like blasphemy, heresy, witchcraft, treason and assassinations require a tribunal. Such serious religious crimes should be tried here by the parish tribunal of the priest, the Canon-theologian, that is I myself and thirdly, the senior administrator of the local church, the Abbess Concordee.

GARZON: *(to the Abbess)* My dear Abbess, your concern for a solution to this mystery is inspiring.

ABBESS: *(smiling inscrutably)* I am just a poor old lady at heart. It's the traditional role of the Abbess to represent her nuns and the local poor. *(humbly)* After all, I must help to protect the flock of local hard-working, honest, religious people who fish and shoot waterfowl for a living. I try to preserve our local culture and also protect the poor from the powers of darkness. That's why I study here. *(indicates open books and the bookshelves)* Of course, my first duty is to direct the religious community of nuns - the convent.

O'Neill is interested and nods then looks curiously at some of the books.

O'NEILL: Indeed Abbess, so I see. You are engaged in deep theology . . hmm . . St. John Chrysostom, St. Augustine - all very orthodox and praiseworthy, I'm sure.

ABBESS: *(pleased)* Thank you, Mr. O'Neill.

There is a sound of scuffling and shouting off-stage. **Enter the Sisters Papillion and Prudence,** *bowing to the Abbess.*

PAPILLION: The constable has arrived with a lost sister.

***Enter Sergeant Antoine**, swarthy, mature-aged, with black hair and white teeth. He is **pushing Doloree,** hands tied behind her back. Antoine is bumbling and officious, dressed in military fashion.*

SERGEANT: *(pushing Doloree ahead of him)* The guilty one has been found. I myself discovered the hiding place in an old boathouse - surrounded by cats. *(abusively to Doloree)* Rider of broomsticks, changer into cats *(thinks, scratches head)* No . . dogs. We have you now, witch . . brewer of magic stew . . .

DOLOREE: *(naively)* Lies, lies, all lies . . such terrible lies.

ABBESS: *(imperiously)* Silence, Antoine, it is for the Mother Superior, not you, to decide this sister's guilt or innocence.

Antoine pauses, bows obsequiously, remembers to remove his hat.

SERGEANT: Indeed, your superiorness. Forgive my enthusiasm, ma'am and gentlemen. You see it's my duty as an honest policeman.

ABBESS: *(interrupting)* Quiet, Sergeant. You may leave. This sister is now back in her rightful home. It is our decision that you leave. Is that not so, Canon Louis?

CANON: *(twitching negatively, No, No)* Yes, oh, yes indeed, Mother Superior.

Antoine backs out, bowing and scraping the floor, showing his teeth, but it's not clear if he is sincere or sarcastic. The Abbess watches him carefully as he withdraws.

SERGEANT: *(leaving)* Thank you for taking over, Canon. Put her to death! She's guilty . . a witch . . she scratched me . . on the nose . . kill her off . . like a dog . . she's a wolf dog . . a scratching witch . . . *(points towards Doloree with his hat)*

Sergeant Antoine leaves the stage left.

DOLOREE: No, No, I'm not a witch. I'm not guilty. I've done no harm. I've hurt no one.

ABBESS: Prudence, my dear Prudence, bring Pierre here at once. He's one of our historians on witches and heresy. *(to Mr. O'Neill)* Pierre is curator of our museum. *(points to the pictures on the left wall)* He's very much an expert on the local workings of the inquisition and how to deal with possible apostates.

Prudence bows and leaves.

O'NEILL: *(astounded and incredulous)* Witches?   Surely, if this poor woman had supernatural powers she would have wounded the sergeant with more than a scratched nose?

ABBESS: *(superstitiously cautious)* It is said that the strength of a werewolf comes and goes according to such things as spells and potions and movements of the moon and stars. We must be careful. We do know that Sister Doloree had at least deserted the Abbey.

Enter Prudence and Pierre. Pierre is hunchbacked, thick set and weak-faced, pale but cheerful, powerful, soulless, dressed in a curator's uniform with cap and thick waist belt. He struts, not walks. He is arrogant and self-confident on the surface but fragile and fearsome underneath.

PIERRE: Mother Superior, Canon, ladies and gentlemen I am at your service. *(bows)*

ABBESS: *(pointing to Doloree)* Sister Doloree has been absent from the Abbey without permission and so is a suspect in certain crimes. Your knowledge of the crimes and apostasies of oldentimes may be of help here.

Pierre bows again and kneels on one knee beside Doloree, who holds her bound hands behind her back. Doloree holds her head low, still kneeling.

ABBESS: Doloree my child - a poor woman was killed last night. She was Matilde, the priest's mother. You were seen at the priest's house speaking to Matilde at the time when she was killed. This was no ordinary murder to be tried at common court. This was a murder by a witch or wizard, for the form of the werewolf was seen. Divine laws may well have been broken. So we must find out if you are guilty or have any information about the murder. Do you understand?

PRUDENCE: *(laughing and chortling, pointing to the three nooses outside the window)* See the lovely view from our little museum.

PAPILLION: *(rubbing her hands together with keenness)* Yes, and those old pictures may also encourage you to tell what's true - hee, hee, hee - give us a clue.

O'Neill glances unpleasantly at the sisters and at the pictures of the inquisition and the three nooses hanging in the courtyard, outside the window.

DOLOREE: Mother Superior, I understand that these killings are the work of demons and wizards. But I know nothing of them. I'm just an old nurse. All last night I was attending a sick-bed several miles away from the house of the priest where this terrible murder took place. I know nothing of the murder. I've never murdered anyone. Someone must have been pretending to be me. I'm innocent. Please, Mother, you are the only protector of us poor religious in these remote swamplands and jungles, please let me be sent back to my work.

The Abbess makes no response and Doloree continues desperately.

The sick ones I visited are witnesses for me that I was there with them last night - I wasn't even near the house of Father Charles – it's ten miles away. I was told by the family of the sick that I was a suspect and the police were looking for me. So I hid nearby - in fear - not guilt.

O'NEILL: That's easily checked on. We will do so.

ABBESS: *(pleasantly)* One moment, Mr. O'Neill, this is our responsibility, not yours. Let our usual inquiry process be observed. We have local contacts and will pass all findings on to you.

O'NEILL: *(looking surprised and upset but self-controlled)* Of course.

GARZON: My dear Abbess, if anyone in the world can help, it will be Mr. Felix O'Neill, the world's greatest consulting detective.

ABBESS: *(diplomatically)* We understand that you are here to help, Mr. O'Neill. However, our local law requires that where the testimony of the accused differs from that of the accuser then the accused must be put to a test.

DOLOREE: No, No, No. There's no reason. Why can't my witnesses be called to testify?

ABBESS: *(smoothly but hostily)* Doloree, your witnesses will be called, my dear. But you are making things difficult for us. You will also be questioned and soon.

DOLOREE: Oh, no. Not that.

O'NEILL: *(puzzled, concerned and suspicious)* Not what?

ABBESS: *(to Pierre)* Take her to the old museum, to the Chamber of Confessions and keep her there, *(she raises her finger in caution)* but do not question her.

Pierre shakes his head, absently.

PIERRE:　No, No.　I would never do that, Mother Superior.　It's not for me to question a religious.

ABBESS:　*(pointing to Papillion and Prudence)* Dear sisters, you should speak to her about these inconsistencies between her story and those of the priest and Elene who say that they saw Doloree last night in the presbytery when the priest's mother was murdered.

The Sisters Papillion and Prudence smile and bow.　Pierre pulls Doloree almost off left stage. She screams and resists, but he pushes and pulls her by the arms.
Exit Pierre and Doloree.

O'NEILL:　What's going on here?　Where exactly are you taking this woman?

The Abbess is silent and contemptuous.

ABBESS:　Merely to the old museum - a mere reminder of the church's ability to find out the truth in times past.

CANON:　*(twitching, No, No)* The normal process it to interrogate and persuade suspects to tell the truth.　We can't just take their word that they are innocent and then release them. They must be subject to some kind of inquisitional justice. Of course we cannot and would not use force today but we can use a little psychology – to, perhaps, just look at the former implements of truth seeking.

GARZON: *(horrified)* I hope you don't mean some form of intimidation. Surely you can't mean threats or scares? An old woman would confess to anything under threat.

O'Neill nods but remains cool and suspicious.

ABBESS: *(to O'Neill and Garzon)* No, of course we don't mean threats - just a subtle reminder.

PRUDENCE: *(bowing and squirming)* Thank you, Mother Superior.

(to O'Neill) Thank you. We will take care of our sister. Our gentle sisters alone will inquire of her concerning these matters.

ABBESS: My dear gentlemen, you must understand that here we have a traditional, rural setting. I remind you that this is all within my personal jurisdiction as an Abbess.

O'NEILL: Of course Abbess, we're not questioning your responsibilities.

ABBESS: *(continues)* There have been horrible murders, apparently a werewolf, certainly cold blooded killing. People respond to the traditional procedures - just as Doloree responded just now - with fear so that actual torture is never necessary. The old torture machines are only a tourist and student attraction - at most a psychological threat - never used in reality.

The others nod in agreement.

O'NEILL: I certainly hope not.

ABBESS: *(evasively)* All that is needed is the fear of the consequences of lying and what do we get? We get what we want, what you want, what all of human civilization has sought for centuries, all that we need for justice and honor and for the making of an orderly life so that the good can live freely and the wicked can be punished, all that we need for civilization to continue - the truth.

O'NEILL: Yes, we do indeed want the truth.

ABBESS: My dear Mr. O'Neill and Dr. Garzon, we could not, we simply could not get this truth - the truth - simply by asking for it. We need to work for it, perhaps by craft, by cunning, even by trickery. Maybe, alas, by some slight, some little white deception at times but in any case, by all means possible to get at that truth - so that justice can be achieved.

O'NEILL: But we need to get it in a way that people can respect.

ABBESS: *(dreamily and intently, as one seeing visions)* Justice can only be reached through the road to *truth*. Justice is the result of truth and can only be achieved by hard work - it doesn't come easily. So let's not condemn the traditional ways of finding out the truth.

GARZON: But those old machines that you show Doloree, whether they work or not, whether in a museum or not were once used to harm people and cause pain. Is this a good image for a body of religious, a community of prayer?

ABBESS: Mr. O'Neill and Dr. Garzon, I have here many volumes written by the saints. They flogged themselves and had themselves flogged to come to a knowledge of the truth. The greatest saints in the history of the church. Shall I recall their lives to you?

O'NEILL: *(sharply)* No, ma'am. I am quite aware of the voluntary self-discipline of the early saints but this is not self-discipline nor is it voluntary.

ABBESS: *(a little taken back)* No, but we try to find out what really happened not by traditional methods but by a reminder of such. This is better than merely asking malefactors to voluntarily admit their crimes. Surely you don't believe in merely asking them, Are you a murderer? Answer No. Very well, you are free to go. Surely there must be more to it than this. Remember, we are a <u>remote</u> religious community, we don't have scientific laboratories to sift evidence, analyze soil or blood or bones or skin. We need some kind of objectivity.

O'NEILL: Well, yes. You need impartial evidence. Good, objective witnesses, for instance.

ABBESS: And if these aren't forthcoming, what then? The killer walks free? Please bear with us gentlemen.

O'NEILL: Look, Abbess, I am here only on the invitation of a person who wishes to remain unnamed, an investigator, I do hope that I can help you all to achieve the safety and the law and order you wish to achieve. Please grant me one favor.

ABBESS: *(pleasantly)* But of course Mr. O'Neill. I too wish to restore law and order. What is your favor? Would you and Dr. Garzon wish to be our guests here at the abbey?

O'NEILL: Thank you but I need to be among the poor people, the victims, to receive information.   But if you would, promise me that no one will be charged or accused until I have had a chance, with others help no doubt, to find out by proper evidence and witnesses just what is going on here and who or what is responsible.

ABBESS: You have my promise, Mr. O'Neill. Some persons may need to be . . ah . . counseled a little . . for that is the established disciplinary practice here but I can certainly promise you that no one will come to harm within my jurisdiction until they have been counseled in front of impartial witnesses.   And you may be in attendance here *(she indicates some chairs)* at any time you wish. You have my word, as Mother Abbess, on this.

O'NEILL: Thank you madam Abbess.   Then, I will waste no more time *(drawing together his cloak, his hat and walking stick)* in trying to help solve these mysteries.   Thank you for your courtesy.

ABBESS: *(smiling and shaking hands with Felix O'Neill and Dr. Garzon)* And I will look forward to hearing of your progress. Goodbye gentlemen. *(in a relaxed and leisurely way)*

O'NEILL: *(leaving, bowing)* Goodbye, Abbess.

O'Neill and Dr. Garzon leave stage left.

VOICE OF DOLOREE: *(from off stage)* NO, NO, I've never killed. I'm not a witch.

CURTAIN

ACT TWO
Who is the Werewolf?

Scene One:
The Werewolf Analyzed

The scene takes place outside the church sub-set that runs from left to right stage at the back of the graveyard (see Act One, Scene One). Most of the action takes place in the center part of this area in the churchyard at the front of the church but to the right of the crypt which is set below the level of the church. Most of the lighting will be on the area of action with some shadowy lighting purely for setting and atmosphere on the abbey and the priest's house.

    Enter from right Felix O'Neill and his friend Dr. Garzon. They meet at the front of the church. Mr. O'Neill is dressed as before. The men wear hats which they remove. They both retain their traveling cloaks and walking sticks. The mature-aged Dr. Garzon is now wearing a white suit, white shirt and bow tie.

Enter Madame Vermillion and finds a quiet place to sit. She is young, alert, light in build and size, short-sighted with glasses, intellectual and eccentric-looking as one who is sharp and knowledgeable in the life sciences. She is a keen enthusiastic person who is continually taking off her glasses, wiping and adjusting them. Professor Vermillion meets with Dr. Garzon and Mr. O'Neill as by prior arrangement. They greet and shake hands as they talk quietly in front of the church, a little overclouded by the eerie atmosphere of the graves and the rumble of thunder.

GARZON: *(to Professor Vermillion)* I'm Dr. Garzon, healtharian and homeopath and also a former health officer in the mercantile marine. *(pointing at each in turn)* This is my friend Felix O'Neill, a professor of forensic science and a master detective.

O'Neill shakes his head and smiles at Vermillion as if to say – there he goes again. They all shake hands. Garzon continues to speak.

Like Madame Vermillion, I'm also researching for a novel of the supernatural. It seems we're both interested in the occult but I'm more into the spiritual approach to witchcraft although novels essentially provide entertainment and amusement.

O'NEILL: Well, of course, novels are more than fun. Some novelists predict, others inform, some are scientific, some change society.

VERMILLION: On the other hand, science also has its myths and honored falsehoods.

O'NEILL: Quite so, I must agree Madame la Professeur.

VERMILLION: *(looking up at the sky, in awe)* Sky grumble.

GARZON: *(puzzled)* Beg pardon, Ma'am?

VERMILLION: Localspeak for thunder and drums – a bad day for the fearful.

GARZON: Yes, alas for the fearful victims but my friend O'Neill is probably the world's greatest detective. His brain and his intuitive powers are second to none. The killer's days are drawing to a close.

O'NEILL: My dear Garzon as usual you exaggerate my skills.

GARZON: We'll soon see about that O'Neill. As I was saying, I'm also interested in the humanitarian and healing aspects of any discipline. That's why I thought we should meet here beside the church because many of the appearances and attacks of the werewolf have taken place in the homes and roads near this old graveyard. *(points around center stage)*

O'NEILL: I seek a scientific and non-magical explanation of why this old graveyard should be involved. I'm investigating primarily to meet an intellectual challenge but also to help make this world a better place.

VERMILLION: I'm interested in the strange and unusual in natural science. One of my recent interests is pathology. The man-wolf may be a pathological mutant and this is a rare chance to study one so extraordinary.

O'NEILL: So you study freaks?

VERMILLION: Well . . yes . . the freak represents the sick man of creation. What makes its mind work? Why does it do as it does? Some scientists only want to understand the way individuals survive. I seek to lay foundations for the ultimate healing of many in order to set the whole man in a healthy world and that necessitates the study of genetic deviants.

Anyway, I'm very pleased to meet both of you. It's good to know that I'm not the only one investigating these mysterious werewolf murders. Let's share our knowledge and suspicions for just a moment.

O'NEILL: *(visibly pleased)* Absolutely, we may learn from each other, professor.

VERMILLION: Yes, I understand that both of you have visited the local Abbey.

O'NEILL: Indeed, and you may be interested to know that I've already checked out Doloree's alibi this afternoon. Several persons have told me that she was visiting the sick some miles away at the time of the murder but the priest's housekeeper and servants are adamant that Doloree was there at the time of the murder of the priest's mother.

VERMILLION: Ah, there is a mystery here that needs investigating.

O'NEILL: Well, I've been working on a theory for some time and the fact of Doloree being in two places at the same time appears to confirm my theory.

VERMILLION: What theory, Mr. O'Neill?

O'NEILL: *(continues)* Well . . according to our

known science it's impossible to impersonate anyone in appearance and voice and personality to such an extent as to fool old friends but I believe that werewolves are advanced masters in the arts of disguise.

GARZON: This sounds incredible O'Neill.

O'NEILL: It's just unbelievable that the werewolf would reveal its true identity so easily as to call at someone's front door as Doloree did, be identified by several good witnesses and then murder someone. *(deliberately and coldly)* So, it follows that the person acting as Doloree, a harmless old nun and nurse, was someone or something else.

In fact, I'm sure that disguise is the key to the mystery and not merely ordinary disguise but a high level of metamorphosis or shapeshifting.

VERMILLION: Mr. O'Neill, to me as a scientist, metamorphosis is not an acceptable explanation. It smacks of the supernatural.

O'NEILL: Not at all. It's a very natural process, but, of course, too advanced for scientists of today to quite understand.

VERMILLION: *(pleasantly)* But not too difficult for an imaginative detective to grasp?

O'NEILL: *(ignoring the irony)* Exactly. Creative investigators and writers are always eras ahead of scientists.

Vermillion raises her eyebrows, shrugs and wipes her glasses.

GARZON: Well, O'Neill, my dear fellow, in my superficial studies of sorcery and witchcraft, I've come across those who would sell their soul to the devil in order to gain power over others.

O'NEILL: This all points to my theory that here we deal with a shapeshifter. I fear that the werewolf is a master of murderous disguise who peddles a deadly and diabolical delusion.

VERMILLION: Dr. Garzon, with all due regard to your religious beliefs and, Mr. O'Neill, with every respect to your scientific analysis and strong investigative imagination, can I humbly just point out that there is a disease of the genes, known as lycanthropy or werewolfism. Also, it's been well established that the full moon exercises a tyrannical power over the minds and bodies of humans.

O'NEILL: *(calmly)* Why?

VERMILLION: *(at a loss)* Why? Why? Why, because it's a time when the mind is weak.

O'NEILL: Really? So, when the wolfman's mind is weak - he turns into a wolf, a very strong animal. How can that be?

VERMILLION: Now you, Mr. O'Neill, are into mere theory - for your so-called science has never been accepted by any scientific school and you, sir, Dr. Garzon, are into magic, but my explanation, lycanthropy, is a known inherited disease.

GARZON: *(shaking his head in disapproval)* The wolfman is a child of devilry, not a chance mismatch of nature. The Good Book says, "Beware of false prophets in sheep's clothing but inwardly they are ravening wolves." And again, "ravening wolves will enter in among you, not sparing the flock."

VERMILLION: *(looks at all present and waves her hand to include others unseen)* You realize, Mr. O'Neill, that if there's any truth in your theories at all - and I don't know that there is - that almost anyone could be the werewolf?

O'NEILL: Including you.

VERMILLION: Exactly. *(to O'Neill)* There are a lot of suspects.

O'NEILL: *(spreading his hands)* I never suggested otherwise. *(pointing in a pedagogical way)* All I've suggested is that the werewolf is a creature of advanced science not magic or demons, not a matter of nature or genetic disorder.

GARZON: The devil lies behind all evil and these killings are evil. I feel sure that the selling of souls, with his sorcery and magic is the basis of the terror.

VERMILLION: I'm not so sure, as a clinical scientist, I wouldn't completely dismiss any possibility either magic or shapeshifting but I do suspect that a simple natural explanation is going to prove to be the answer to the mystery. We need to remember that lycanthropy has been accepted for many centuries as a disease, the man-wolf syndrome – a form of chimera by natural dysfunction.

O'NEILL: Then why are there not similar mistakes with fish or fowl or cats or horses. All this is mere mythology. So you're both wrong, as educated people - minds on rails - usually are.

VERMILLION: I was thinking that before we hear any witnesses we should remember that three people run this town - the Abbess, the Priest and the Canon. Indeed the three are just about all of law and order in this village. If we're going to achieve any kind of justice or honest solution to the werewolf mystery, we'll need their help.

O'NEILL: Do you mean for purposes of getting cooperation from the public – the help would be dubious I suspect.

GARZON: Well, O'Neill, perhaps up to a point. What Professor Vermillion *(he bows to the lady)* suggests may have some validity. However, *(lowers his voice and glances around)* the Canon is on his way and he is hardly the strongest personality - unless he's a great actor and fooling us, *(sotto)* . . Speak of the devil . . .

Enter Canon Louis and Sergeant Antoine.

CANON: *(shaking his head and twitching, No, it can't be true)* My compliments. How are you all?

O'NEILL: Very well, sir. We were just discussing the events among ourselves.

CANON: *(twitching, No, No)* I had a witness before my court who gave testimony about one of these murders. Her name is Blanche. As you know I'm also the Coroner. *(shrugs and looks mystified and then twitches)* Sergeant Antoine, you also heard her testimony in court, isn't that so?

SERGEANT: *(blankly)* I don't remember, sir. To tell you the truth, I'm only here to arrest people, if that's what you want, your honor. *(stands back, and spreads his hands and grins broadly)* Show me the villain, murderer, werewolf suspect, creature of terror and I'll seize him. *(growls and strangles an imaginary suspect)*

Trust me, ma'am, sirs, your honor, I would arrest my own mother if ordered to. Although that would somewhat upset me *(looks sad)* since I have almost forgiven her for my upbringing and I still *(as one in great generosity of spirit)* . . . I still retain some small glimmer of liking for the ugly old hag. *(hand on heart)* Yes, I still almost feel a little soft spot for her, despite all that she did to me growing up.

Yes, I would arrest anyone *(laughs)* including any of the four of you. Ha, Ha, Ha - just joking but true all the same, ha, ha.

CANON: *(with a shrug and distaste)* In my work I find people like you, Sergeant, necessary but revolting.

SERGEANT: *(bowing and grinning)* Thank you, thank you, your honor. *(touches his temple)* I appreciate the compliment. *(modestly)* I do my best, yessir, I do my best, sir, to be, as you say, revolting against the ancient regime. Vive la republique!

Canon looks mystified and twitches while the others stare at each other and shake their heads in wonderment at his comments.

CURTAIN

ACT TWO
Who is the Werewolf?

Scene Two:
An Eyewitness Talks

Enter Anne *the Hotel Manager,* **with Blanche***, a solemn young girl, in long servant's clothes, shy and nervous. Blanche bows and curtsies to the company and frowns unhappily. Sergeant kisses hand of Anne and raises his hat extravagantly.*

ANNE: This is Blanche. *(kindly and coaxingly)* Blanche you're among friends, so please relax. I believe they'd like to know the full story of the murder incident - just as you told it to me.

They all nod in approval.

CANON: *(twitching negatively, No, No, definitely not, No, No)* Yes Anne, the girl was clearly shocked. It's time now to hear the whole story from the beginning.

Blanche relaxes somewhat but still looks unhappy.

BLANCHE: If I thought I was going to be believed I wouldn't hesitate to . . *(looks at Canon guiltily)* fill in some *(she looks down)* details.

CANON: *(resignedly but not unkindly)* Very well, child. Let's hear your fully detailed story . . better late than never. *(twitches again)* We just want to hear all the facts. Please tell.

BLANCHE: *(hesitatingly)* This may show that Doloree was not the werewolf.

CANON: Well, that may be but Doloree has already confessed.

VERMILLION: *(shaking her head sadly)* Only under threats I fear.

O'NEILL: Or worse, under torture perhaps.

ANNE: *(to Blanche)* Blanche, please tell them what you told me.

BLANCHE: *(at the point of tears)* Let me pull myself together first. *(pauses, puts her head in her hands, kneels down in mental turmoil)* It was the day Michel and I thought would be as happy as any in our lives. We were in love. We went deep into the forest, just the two of us and Bobbin our little pack-donkey to pluck wild fruit and berries. Eventually we ended up in this old churchyard where many dread to go due to fear of the dead.

O'NEILL: Blanche, did you see or hear anyone else when you came into the graveyard?

BLANCHE: No sir, there was only the two of us as far as I know.

ANNE: Take your time Blanche. What you have to tell is very important.

BLANCHE: It was near noonday. Michel began to feel tired so he lay down among some shaded bushes while I walked off to pluck some flowers. I was never more than forty or fifty yards away from him at the most. Though I could not see him, I knew that he was resting nearby, so I wasn't afraid.

VERMILLION: You didn't see or hear anyone else while you were picking the flowers?

BLANCHE: No, I'm quite sure there wasn't anyone else around. It was very quiet with just a few birds singing in the treetops. Just as I began to feel really pleased with my bouquet, suddenly the sounds of terror pierced my ears. Birds cried out and squirrels screeched in fear. I heard the howling and growling of a dog or wolf and the screams of Michel coming from the place where he lay resting.

O'NEILL: Blanche, what did you do?

BLANCHE: I dropped the flowers and screamed "Michel are you all right?" At first I was petrified. I couldn't move. Then I heard Michel cry "Blanche, the gun, get the gun . . the gun . . ."

His voice was overwhelmed by the wolf sounds as I ran to our donkey and seized the old shotgun out of the saddlebag. I ran back towards the scene of the attack. From the ravening and growling noises and shouts I knew that Michel had at least been seriously wounded and I was determined to save him, if I could. I slowly walked towards the place of the attack, pointing the gun.

O'NEILL: Tell us exactly what you saw next?

BLANCHE: Suddenly, the figure of Michel rose up out of the whinbushes, almost like one walking on air. I was terrified. He seemed so calm, so deadly calm and relaxed. Even the birds became silent. I heard a swishing sound like a cloak or skirts moving and I smelt a strange herbal smell in the air. I stopped and pointed the gun at the apparition - for at that time I felt sure it was Michel's ghost because it spoke to me so calmly. He just kept saying Blanche, put down that gun. It's only me, Michel. What's the matter? Put away the gun please.

GARZON: Did you?

BLANCHE: No sir. I just couldn't believe that Michel hadn't heard the screaming. He looked at me strangely and beckoned to me with his left hand.
Come here, Blanche. Give me the gun, don't shoot. I'm unharmed. All is well.

O'NEILL: Did you give him the gun?

BLANCHE: No sir. I didn't know what to do. He was so calm and smiled at me. The birds were still silent. I just couldn't believe that he hadn't been harmed so I continued to back off and kept pointing the gun at him or his apparition. He kept strangely moving towards me and saying, Come here Blanche. There's nothing wrong. Why are you pointing that gun at me?

VERMILLION: What did you do Blanche?

BLANCHE: I backed off onto the country road near the Abbey and fortunately the sergeant was passing at that time and he asked me what was the matter and could he help.

SERGEANT: She was in shock. I tried to calm her and then we went to view the place where Michel had been sleeping.

BLANCHE: Truly, the image of Michel that spoke to me had been a fantasy. For even as I had feared, we found not only Michel dead but his body torn to pieces and flung apart by a wild animal, destroyed and half devoured by a wolf or other wild creature. He'd been so handsome. It's become a complete and total nightmare to me.

Blanche becomes very quiet and bows her head and cries as the others look thoughtful and nod understandingly to each other.

O'NEILL: Blanche, can you remember how long it was from the time you saw Michel beckoning to you until you and Sergeant Antoine found his body?

BLANCHE: A few minutes only.

O'NEILL: Sergeant Antoine, what do you think?

SERGEANT: How can I tell? I dunno. All I know is, I was on the horse on routine guard patrol. I heard a great cry from the birds that hoot and call and then I see Blanche with a gun walking backwards. I stop the horse. She cries werewolf and murder and I follow her and I see a body torn up *(shakes his head)* a tragedy of horror - *(shrugs)* - little pieces - someone - no doubt Michel well and truly destroyed. If only it had been my mother instead, I could have breathed more easily but no *(bitterly)* it was an innocent person. Surely this proves my point that Destiny cannot exist. It's just a myth.

CANON: *(solemnly and vindictively)* Blasphemy is still an offense in this country Sergeant Antoine. Are you aware of this?

SERGEANT: *(flamboyantly waving his arms)* Everybody in this village is an atheist except those who make a living from the status quo.

O'NEILL: *(curiously)* What exactly do you mean by status quo?

SERGEANT: The land-owning and government payroll status quo, Mr. O'Neill. What other status quo is there? *(defiantly shouting)* This country is a commonwealth. I am an atheist. It is my right. We are not under the ancient regime. Why should I be interrogated in this way?

O'NEILL: Please don't misunderstand me I wasn't interrogating you Sergeant Antoine. I ask only as an outsider - for information. Now I know that land-owning or taking a government payout *(counts on his fingers)* these things equal the status quo, in this swampland, right?

SERGEANT: That's it, sir, land and government contracts that's corruption - the status quo. Look, I'm sorry. I'm on edge. I worry about these werewolf murders. The body of Michel destroyed, tore me apart just as much as the werewolf tore him apart. *(shakes his head)* We must catch this werewolf and kill it.

It's a tragedy. No one ever deserved to be torn apart in that way *(considers for a moment, rubs his chin ruminatively)* except maybe my mother *(brightening)* but then, ha, ha, retribution will come to her also, if life is just. *(thinks, becomes sad and despondent again)* But then life is not only not just – it's not even good - so what good is that? *(spreads hands and looks miserable)* It's all a mess. A terrible mess.

Professor Vermillion looks at Sergeant Antoine with interest, a long look up and down, just as a zoologist might look at a specimen.

VERMILLION: Hmm . . .

SERGEANT: Lady professor, what's the problem?

VERMILLION: *(changing her attention to Blanche)* I'm just wondering how to explain the apparition of Michel immediately after his murder.

O'NEILL: Yes, I wonder about that. The few seconds between his appearance and the finding of his body would hardly have been enough time to allow for such a terrible murder and mutilation and cannibalism. Therefore, Michel was dead when he appeared to Blanche. Besides, he appeared to her after an apparent vicious werewolf attack, so who was the actor impersonating him? Obviously it was the murderer for I don't believe in ghosts.

SERGEANT: *(eagerly)* No, me either, sir *(nods)* It's bad enough to be scared by them, without having to believe in them.

The Canon twitches negatively at the Sergeant who salutes him, defiantly.

O'NEILL: *(slowly)* Therefore, since dead and mutilated men can't stand up - it wasn't *(as Blanche sobs)* Michel who stood up.

BLANCHE: It preyed on my mind and I brooded on it. I told only my friends and Anne insisted that it could be an important clue to finding out who is the werewolf. So maybe I wasn't insane at the time?

ANNE: Yes, it certainly could be a clue Blanche - If the Michel you saw wasn't really himself, then perhaps the Doloree who was seen at the time of the werewolf murder of Matilde, may not have been the true Doloree.

GARZON: *(worried)* Still, it doesn't tell us the identity of the werewolf.

O'NEILL: No, but if we know that the old nun is probably not the werewolf, then we know to look for someone else urgently before another murder proves the point for us.

BLANCHE: That's my reason for telling what is so hard to explain. More than anything I wish to bring the murderer of Michel to justice. I now feel sure that I saw the werewolf in disguise. There's no other real explanation. As you say, Mr. O'Neill, what I saw couldn't have been Michel.

CANON: But you said that at first you thought it was his ghost. Hmm. Yes, that's it. The apparition appeared after Michel's death. Therefore, it must have been his ghost. Yes, Yes. *(twitches, No, No)*

Professor Vermillion and Dr. Garzon look puzzled and uneasy.

ANNE: *(tearfully)* But why would his ghost be so untroubled after what happened?

O'NEILL: *(astounded and unable to control himself)* Yes, why should Michel's ghost say that all was well after his body had just been torn apart by a werewolf. Also, Canon, why would a ghost be afraid of a gun?

CANON: *(looking embarrassed and twitching, No, No, No and turning to Sergeant Antoine for an escape)* Strange how you just happened to be there at the time, Sergeant. Hmm . . self-confessed skeptic, perhaps into magic and Satanism. Mm . . *(he scratches his chin)* very suspicious. *(looks Sergeant up and down)*

SERGEANT: *(horrified)* Me, Rev. Canon? Me? Oh, Reverend, I'm only exercising my democratic rights to be a mother-hating, faith-denyer. Motherhood and Faith went out with the old world. *(straightening up)* I'm a true revolutionary. You try making trouble for me, and I swear, I swear, I will provoke an international constitutional crisis. I stand on my secular rights . . against the foreigners. I'll appeal to the governor. I'll . .

ANNE: *(whispering)* Please be calm, Sergeant Antoine, we don't doubt your patriotism.

SERGEANT: Thank you Miss Anne *(he seems relieved and appeased)* I try to do my best to represent the people. *(he salutes flamboyantly)* No established church, no privileged classes, no land-owning establishment. No firing squads . . at least not without due process of law. *(he salutes again)* Firing squads and nooses - that is not the freedom.

CANON: *(twitching, No, No)* Yes, Yes, very patriotic, Sergeant. *(in disgust)* very egalitarian and fraternal and libertarian.

GARZON: *(to Blanche, kindly)* Your story is very important, my dear. It means that there's delusion and magic involved in these mysterious werewolf murders. We can't just blame anyone seen near the scene of the crime after what you've told us.

O'NEILL: Blanche, thank you for telling what must bring back unhappy thoughts. The worst is that the killer should be given his freedom to continue these horrific murders. It's important that you should explain your vision to the Abbess and Fr. Charles, for they're also concerned with justice in the parish.

BLANCHE: The Abbess and Fr. Charles control the great lands of the church.

CANON: So what, my child? There's nothing wrong with land ownership, is there?

BLANCHE: Oh no, it's just that I'm so unimportant I'm afraid to visit them.

ANNE: *(to Blanche)* Well, maybe you could at least tell your story to Fr. Charles.

BLANCHE: I suppose I must talk to Fr. Charles. The truth is a terrible thing.

O'NEILL: No truer words were ever spoken, my dear Blanche. The truth exposes not only persons but civilizations, nothing is more dangerous than the truth. And many persons, for their own reasons, wish to suppress it.

The others nod in agreement.

O'NEILL: We'll arrange a meeting at some quiet place for you to meet Fr. Charles. Why not in the church right here?

Dr. Garzon puts his arms around Blanche's shoulders, protectfully.

GARZON: I'll escort you back to the Inn afterwards - that's a promise.

BLANCHE: *(brightening)* Very well, Dr. Garzon. I trust you so I'll talk to the priest.

ANNE: *(to Blanche)* I think we've made our contribution for now. Let's get back to the Inn.

Exit right Blanche and Anne. *The Sergeant bows to Anne as she leaves.*

CURTAIN

ACT TWO
Who is the Werewolf?

Scene Three:
Blanche's Testimony Discussed
Same scene as before in the churchyard.

GARZON: But what does it all prove?

O'NEILL: Blanche's story proves that the "demon" or werewolf was afraid of a gun. It proves that the werewolf wasn't a ghost but a mortal - one of us - perhaps you *(looks all around)* or me but certainly a mortal.

CANON: *(twitches negatively)* I take the point that the werewolf may, I say, may be able to adopt disguises and delude people but on the other hand illusions are well known to occur at the time of death.

VERMILLION: Yes, Canon, but such death-bed illusions are usually seen by the dying person only, not others.

CANON: Yes, Madame Vermillion, as you say, usually, but not quite always. Occasionally, others see and hear the Banshee or beckoning ghost or whatever, at the time of death.

VERMILLION: Such phenomena are mere mass schizophrenia, if you ask me.

CANON: Be that as it may, Doloree has made a full confession and signed it.

GARZON: Under fear and duress. Surely such a confession can't be acceptable evidence.

CANON: That will not be for me but for a secular tribunal to decide.

O'NEILL: Doloree was at a sick-bed when Fr. Charles' mother was murdered. This can be proven by witnesses.

CANON: *(twitching negatively)* We're going around in circles. It remains to be seen whether the testimony of such witnesses holds up under the scrutiny of discipline.

VERMILLION: *(shocked)* You don't mean that you intimidate the witnesses too?

SERGEANT: Intimidation has always been a very popular pastime of the establishment. That's what they're for, to protect the status quo.

CANON: *(angrily)* You're getting quite out of line, Sergeant.

SERGEANT: *(saluting)* Beg pardon, Rev. Canon, I withdraw the remark *(scowling)* but I still support the people.

O'NEILL: I think that Blanche's story proves that the werewolf is a master disguiser and could be anyone. Doloree is just a poor scared old woman whom the werewolf imitated to gain access to the Priest's house.

CANON: I agree that we probably don't know who the werewolf is, at this time, but the case of Doloree serves to strike fear into the hearts of the populace in general and helps to suppress crime. *(twitches uncontrollably, No, No)* It's a well established principle of law and order that it's a good thing to hang a few people now and then and incarcerate as many as possible. Indeed *(twitches again)* it's a public virtue to hang people regularly in order to terrorize the lower criminal elements.

VERMILLION: *(with incredulity)* My ears are cheating me. I don't believe this!

O'NEILL: *(to the Canon, horrified)* But surely you hang only the guilty?

CANON: *(with raised eyebrows and considering)* Well, human justice is imperfect. *(twitches)* But yes I agree with you, I would much <u>prefer</u> to execute only the guilty rather than the not guilty. My Christian conscience compels me to admit this. But while, in an ideal world, one would prefer to hang only the guilty, however *(shrugs)* if the identity of the real villain is not known we must hang somebody, mustn't we? I mean we can't just ignore the crimes and hang no one. That would only encourage more crime, wouldn't it? What do you think?

O'NEILL: *(looking horrified, taking a deep breath to control himself, then speaking slowly and deliberately)* I think the sooner we find and destroy the werewolf, the better it'll be for all the people living in these backward swamps and forests.

The Canon twitches negatively. The Sergeant nods and applauds.

SERGEANT: Yes sir, Mr. O'Neill and don't worry, soon the people will abolish all hangings as mere tools of tyranny.

CANON: *(to the Sergeant)* I doubt it. The ignorant masses just love hangings. Hangings and democracy are brothers. However, Sergeant, our hearing of the witness is over and it's time to go.

Exit Canon followed by Sergeant Antoine.
Sergeant turns, bows and raises hat as he
leaves.

GARZON: It becomes clear that this mystery is more complex, more intractable than we suspected.

O'NEILL: We've just received some valuable clues as to how the werewolf operates in almost supernaturally perfect disguises but how or why or who?

VERMILLION: *(shakes her head)* We'll need to sleep on it but alas with our doors locked.

O'NEILL: *(concurring)* I also suggest with our windows barred.

GARZON: Let's meet here again tomorrow morning for a real scrutiny - a deep look at delusion and evil. I've some ideas of my own that I need to ruminate on tonight.

The other two acquiesce; ***all three exit the***
stage left.

The lights fade slowly on the churchyard, then
dimmer as lights rise again on the center of the
set. The scene is similar to the previous scene in
which Michel rises from among the graveyard

foliage and beckoned to Blanche, except that Michel is now alone. He continues to beckon with his left hand raised to about shoulder level, his face strangely expressionless and mysteriously, as before. Slowly, as Michel continues to beckon...

CURTAIN

ACT TWO
Who is the Werewolf?

Scene Four:
What is a Werewolf

The general tone of this scene is chilly, suspicious and paranoid, culminating in the appearance of the illusory Priest. The audience should be uncertain of his authenticity, i.e., he represents at this point only a mystery, a question mark. Mr. O'Neill, Professor Vermillion and Dr. Garzon are gathering in the churchyard as before in front of the church. This time they walk around and explore the place.

GARZON: *(walking up and down lecturing animatedly)* I'm just wondering what kind of a person uses magic spells. Perhaps, an older man sells his soul to the devil in return for youth and the feeling of well-being that comes with being twenty five. At twenty five anyone can conquer the world but the devil can't be good or deliver on his promises. If he did, he wouldn't be evil. By nature he is the Liar, so he stabs the older man in the back. The rejuvenated must obey the devil and kill for the most cruel master in the universe.

O'NEILL: *(with slight ironic humor, incredulously laughing and slapping Dr. Garzon on the back)* After that effort, old chap, you'll have the nerve to deny that you're a professional entertainer. What an imagination!

VERMILLION: *(in contempt)* Magic! Hah! At least lycanthropy has been known for centuries to be a disease of freaks and these waterways and swamplands are just the place for a person to be born naturally as a part-wolf - a wolfman, a cross between man and the ultimate genetic perversion - the sick man of nature, the werewolf. The evidence of strange flowers and swamp creatures . . genetic turmoil is all around us.

Enter Sergeant Antoine. The group and the Sergeant greet each other. The Sergeant bows and then takes up a central position near where the Professor, the Doctor and O'Neill are walking.

SERGEANT: *(raises his left hand in a gesture of despair)* My work is so difficult! I must arrest the innocent *(shakes his head)* It's just too easy to blame these horrible murders on some old ugly witch-like woman like my mother, she didn't do it I'm sure so it would serve no purpose. Still, who cares about mothers? Ugh! No good.

O'NEILL: We know it. But an old nun was seen, to all appearances, at the presbytery when Matilde was murdered. That's one of the reasons why we believe that a shapeshifter is at work and there's the testimony of Blanche.

SERGEANT: Shapeshifter? A what? Who is that? *(afraid and looks around)*

O'NEILL: We're still arguing about the how, the why and who but one thing we are mostly agreed on - a shapeshifter is walking among us.

SERGEANT: A shapeshifter? *(looks at the others as though begging them to deny it)* Is this true?

Dr. Garzon and the others nod.

VERMILLION: *(at a loss to deny it)* It looks to be so. How it comes about exactly, nature or magic or science, those are the three big questions.

SERGEANT: But who could possibly be the villain? I mean the suspects?

GARZON: Anyone, Sergeant. *(indicating the others)* You, me, him or her, anyone. The disguise is so good that we just can't tell.

SERGEANT: But this is horrible. I hate it.

VERMILLION: None of us are above suspicion. However, you Mr. O'Neill or you Dr. Garzon or I myself for that matter, have just arrived and these murders have been going on for some time.

O'NEILL: *(shrugging)* That means nothing. We could have been here before, in disguise. Are we really whom we appear to be? Or perhaps the killings are the work of a murder club and one of us has just joined.

SERGEANT: Please find the shapeshifter or werewolf. Every day that you delay the powers that be grow stronger here. They'll hang anybody just to entertain the poor and prevent a revolt. I fear for my life.

GARZON: Don't worry sergeant, I will personally keep a sharp watch out for you.

SERGEANT: I heard in the village that only a silver bullet can kill a werewolf. *(shrugs and spreads out his hands)*

O'NEILL: Pure superstition, I'm afraid.

GARZON: *(agrees)* Yes, most of the beliefs about the werewolf are just pure superstition.

O'NEILL: My guess would be that a strong bullet from a solid gun would kill it. It's certainly afraid of guns. It's mortal not immortal; flesh not a ghost, ghosts need no food. Supernatural monsters don't fear firearms.

SERGEANT: They say it's a crazy man who turns into a wolf at the full-moon? Zakotu, the villagers call him: an ancient one returned.

VERMILLION: My dear sergeant, whatever name the villagers call it by, it's not as simple as that, I think. No, it's not the usual madman, no ordinary lunatic but someone who deeply studies the occult.

O'NEILL: Certainly, such a person must be close to lunacy, as genius always is close to lunacy. And the full moon may play some small part because it does indeed encourage some minds and passions to acts of violence.

SERGEANT: *(in awe)* Mr. O'Neill, you are a true genius. This is beyond my understanding. You should tell it all to our Priest. Mind you, he holds to some old-fashioned religious beliefs but he is such a wise man in other ways.

O'NEILL: *(pleased at the flattery)* My dear sergeant, Blanche has already agreed to tell her story to the priest. She was afraid of being ridiculed as a criminal fool.

SERGEANT: I'll guarantee her safety from any such charge if she'll just tell Fr. Charles and I'll put a guard on her.

GARZON: But why a guard? The holy cross will surely prove most efficacious against the magic of the werewolf.

O'NEILL: *(irritably)* My dear chap, please . . the cross is only important to those who understand and believe in it. *(raises his index finger)* A mere symbol would hardly intimidate Satan or any truly supernatural creature. There's no guarantee that this particular werewolf is superstitious. Blanche needs a gun not a cross.

SERGEANT: How does this creature make us see it as someone else? Is it the evil eye?

O'NEILL: *(nodding)* Indeed, the eye is the alter

animus - the other soul, perhaps the evil eye is part of the delusion. The evil eye is hypnotic - certainly one should avoid the hypnotic eye but hypnosis is probably only a small part, if any, of the delusion.

VERMILLION: *(sarcastically)* I love this village. It's truly weird. *(to Dr. Garzon)* You believe in magic *(to O'Neill)* you believe in advanced science. Fr. Charles hides. We have been expecting him too long even now. He agreed to meet Blanche but he hides.

GARZON: *(defensively)* Perhaps he's praying in secret. His mother's just been killed, you know.

VERMILLION: *(continuing her tirade)* The Abbess respects various interrogations the way homeopaths believe in remedies. The inhabitants of that Abbey - the nuns - they're about as unique as snow in summer and average 90 years old. Pierre's strange . . obsessed with his museum. The Canon believes in hanging, not as a punishment for the guilty but as an act of public morale building. Sergeant Antoine - he hates his mother! I can't believe that that is compatible with the love of democracy and reform.

SERGEANT: *(laughs and bows)* Just so, Ma'am. *(proudly and strutting out his chest)* I do hate my mother and why not? All men <u>must</u> hate their mothers if they love democracy. Mothers are not democrats.

VERMILLION: *(continuing her tirade and ignoring the sergeant)* No one here is normal. Everyone is a freak but especially you, Mr. O'Neill. You are far too intellectual to be normal.

O'NEILL: *(smiling)* Of course, I forgot, women prefer men to be perhaps just slightly intellectual - clever but never quite clever enough to avoid manipulation and being outwitted by women.

VERMILLION: *(in disgust)* Anyone here could be the werewolf, that's for sure.

O'NEILL: Except you, Professor Vermillion. You are so very normal aren't you?

VERMILLION: Are you sure?

O'NEILL: Oh yes, Professor Vermillion, you and you alone are very, very suspiciously normal.

VERMILLION: What of Anne - the owner of the tavern - a very normal person also? I'm not the only one. *(shrugs, spreads hands, adjusts and cleans her glasses)* Statistically, normal white sheep are bound to occur occasionally, even among the monsters. I'm sorry I'll try harder to be more freakish in future if only to make me feel more at home here.

GARZON: *(laughing heartily)* Among us freakos – ho, ho.

VERMILLION: *(with some contrition, blinks, polishes her glasses, shakes her head, blinking and again adjusting her glasses)* And as for you, Dr. Garzon, your friend has thrown doubt on me because of my supposed normality, my suspicious normality - so you are the prime suspect, according to your lifelong friend.

O'NEILL: *(shocked)* No, I never said so - that's not true!

VERMILLION: Yes, you did – you said normality was suspect. Doctor Garzon said the creature is possibly an older person trying to regain youth by means of werewolfism. No one has greater knowledge of such things than Dr. Garzon, healtharian and homeopath from the internationally acclaimed School of Healthics. If science is the tool of rejuvenation then you may be the rejuvenated one. Come now *(to Dr. Garzon)* who, Dr. Garzon, is better educated in biological science and metaphysics than you, sir?

GARZON: *(laughing and highly flattered)* Coming from a fellow scientist that is a compliment indeed. *(smiles kindly)* However, I can't deny that I know my fields of healthics, herbalism and homeopathy. Thank you, madam. Well yes, maybe so, but *(humbly)* I'm afraid that I'm not your werewolf.

VERMILLION: *(blinking and wiping her glasses)* Indeed, Dr. Garzon. To quote the Abbess and the Canon - do we "just take your word for it?" You're not the only well-educated suspect, of course. The Canon is a lawyer and while lawyers are known for lying, they're not in the least ignorant. The Abbess is no doubt a very learned lady. She supervises an old Abbey and Museum that once dealt with witches and heretics. As such she must be a prima facie suspect. The Priest is also very well versed in the theology of shapeshifting and illusion and knows all about deals with the devil. At the very least a priest has the knowledge to become a werewolf, if knowledge is indeed the key as Mr. O'Neill insists.

O'NEILL: Indeed, I do so insist.

All look at each other suspiciously.

CURTAIN

ACT TWO
Who is the Werewolf?

Scene Five:
What the Priest Thinks

After a pause, **Enter Fr. Charles** *in long black outdoor robes and cape. He is a little awkward and seems not quite at home even in the churchyard. Mr. O'Neill looks at him curiously and suspiciously but greets him respectfully. The others also greet Fr. Charles warmly.*

GARZON: You have suffered a terrible shock, Reverend. *(shaking hands)* All that we said at your mother's funeral holds true. If we can be of any help to you . . .

O'NEILL: If you need any help at the presbytery Rev. Charles, I can send over . . .

FR. CHARLES: Thank you, No . . . Everything is . . in order . . at the presbytery.

VERMILLION: *(tactfully)* We were looking out for you, Reverend . . .

FR. CHARLES: Yes, I've been out visiting parishioners since early . . . Anne has just met with me and asked me to join you.

O'NEILL: Quite. It's just that we're worried that the werewolf murders aren't being properly investigated. Sister Doloree the nun has been suspected because she or someone impersonating her was at the presbytery when your mother was killed.

FR. CHARLES: It was Doloree, I'm sure.

Felix O'Neill looks at him strangely, suspiciously.

O'NEILL: But Fr. Charles, you said at the funeral that you only caught a glimpse of a visitor to your mother.

FR. CHARLES: Oh, yes, well . . perhaps you're right *(strokes his chin)* Maybe I'm clutching after straws. Maybe I'm too anxious to find a culprit . . perhaps I'm a little suffering from shock.

O'NEILL: *(with concern)* We know you've had a great shock but its important to find the true killer. Blanche, the young maid at the Inn, has a story to tell you that seems to show that the werewolf is a cunning master of disguise and probably not Doloree or Sergeant Antoine or anyone else seen near a murder. Can you speak to Blanche and see what you make of her story?

FR. CHARLES: Well, I'm not sure if . . .

O'NEILL: Maybe you can elicit some clue to the killer's identity from your great knowledge of all the people who live here. Neither the Canon, nor the Abbess will pay much heed to three strangers in town, however good our intentions. I'll bring the girl to you personally. I believe her story is part of the proof that the werewolf is a shapeshifter, throwing suspicion on innocent persons by impersonating them at times of murder.

The Priest appears shocked and confused, licks his lips dryly, begins to finger his rosary nervously.

FR. CHARLES: I see . . heavens . . a diabolical impersonator!

GARZON: Father, I'd like to ask you about the werewolf. As you know we're hunting him and hope to capture him.

FR. CHARLES: Yes . . ?

GARZON: When we catch it, the werewolf will not be easy to control. What's the local feeling about how we handle it?

FR. CHARLES: I don't understand . . could you be more specific?

GARZON: Well, can we dispense with a formal trial? Can we just catch it and kill it as a tool of the Devil?

FR. CHARLES: *(uncomfortably)* In theory, yes. *(considers, then looks worried)* In ecclesiastical and civil law a werewolf, whatever it is, is not a Christian or a legal person but either a human follower of the devil or an animal. It's not murder to kill a werewolf. However, in practice, no one person is fit to decide who is or who is not a werewolf or to carry out judgment against a supposed werewolf.

Just as for any other crime, the accused is innocent until proven guilty and is entitled to a fair trial before being condemned to death, so the werewolf must be tried before a higher tribunal of judges - lay or clerical - according to the laws of this parish.

GARZON: I'm sorry Father, but I'd be the last person to go along with that. This is a strange parish indeed. If I see a werewolf all covered with hair and claws - I'm not going to wait for a jury to decide if it was a werewolf that killed me. I'll kill it, before it kills me - that's it.

Priest, twitching his fingers, is unhappy.
FR. CHARLES: I'll be happy to talk to your witness.

GARZON: Blanche, the kitchenmaid, you know her, Reverend but she is nervous and afraid to antagonize the werewolf.

FR. CHARLES: Yes, I know Blanche. She's a truthful girl in general and I'll be happy to hear her story and talk to her at full length about the matter. Of course, this wouldn't be the best time or place - send her to me in the church sometime tomorrow. I'll try to help her or anyone else who may be involved.

O'NEILL: What you'll hear from Blanche may change your mind about the possible guilt of Doloree or Antoine. I'll bring Blanche there to the church *(points to the back sub-set)* at about 10:00 and take her home in person. I'll be well armed to protect her. She's such a frightened little girl. I feel that I must protect her personally.

FR. CHARLES: Fine, Mr. O'Neill - that would be a good time. Ah, Dr. Garzon . . .?

GARZON: Yes . . ?

FR. CHARLES: My son, you surely didn't mean what you said about shooting on sight a mere suspect werewolf?

GARZON: I was never more serious in my life.

FR. CHARLES: I would worry about that, Dr. Garzon.   Please remember your position as a healer - not a destroyer.   Also, it's best to leave it to the judicial system on principle and not to take the law into your own hands.   Of course you have a right of self-defense in special cases.

GARZON: *(unrepentant but respectful, nodding perfunctorily)*   Yes, of course, your reverence.

Priest smiles and counting his rosary - dignified but a little tense and strange.

Fr. Charles leaves stage right.

GARZON: Unless there's more to him than meets the eye.   Is he really just a simple priest? *(in a kindly tone)*

O'NEILL: I think so - but I'm not sure.   Are any of us what we appear to be?   Or are we all something else in disguise?   Now we know that Fr. Charles advocates the constitutional, due process rights of a vicious killer animal.   I'll say one thing for this little village *(bitterly)* it's certainly open to due process and democracy - especially the due process of decapitation and the democracy of death, *(sinisterly)* and nothing is more democratic than death for in the end we all die, don't we?

GARZON: Yes indeed, my dear O'Neill, especially around here.

The company remains on stage, silent and solemn as . . .

CURTAIN

ACT THREE
The Werewolf Triumphs

Scene One:
An Eyewitness is Silenced

Scene is set in the church, Subset Two running down stage from right to left: The crypt of the church left and the sanctuary right. The crypt is sunken below the level of the sanctuary. The crypt of severe and gray colored stone has coffins, pillars, carvings of angels, crosses and other non-denominational Christian symbols. A few steps center lead to right stage which is the sanctuary. The sanctuary is furnished with wooden pews. It has several huge pillars and extreme right a large organ.

As curtain rises, Elene the caretaker's daughter is already lighting candles. *Later she is seen playing the organ in the sanctuary. The organ is at extreme right stage and hidden from the area of the crypt by* *one or more pillars. The sunken location of the crypt also removes it from direct view of the organ. The mood of this scene is mysterious, cold and threatening.*

Blanche enters.

Elene moves from candles to the organ-playing, slow, eerie, traditional music as **Felix O'Neill enters from right,** *the presumed front of church. Blanche is frightened and on tiptoe but he reassures her with a 'relax' gesture.*

BLANCHE: *(timidly raising her voice to a loud whisper)* Fr. Charles, I've come to see you. Father are you there? Fr. Charles?

Elene continues to play strange and eerie music on the organ - Blanche continues in a loud whisper.

Is anyone there? You said you'd meet me here!

Enter the Priest, *in full frock,* **left stage thru the back door of the church** *in the crypt, walks through the crypt and mounts the steps from the crypt so that his head, shoulders and waist are visible to Blanche. His movements are awkward and slow creating suspicion that he may not be the real Priest. O'Neill nods and smiles to Blanche encouragingly and ushers her* *towards the Priest.*

__O'Neill leaves the stage right__ where he entered. The Priest beckons to Blanche with his left hand raised to shoulder level to join him in the crypt. Looking around, hesitantly, she slowly and reluctantly crosses the sanctuary and enters the crypt. The Priest retreats to join her on the stone floor of the crypt then takes Blanche's hand.

FR. CHARLES: *(voice is kindly and reassuring)* Blanche, how nice to see you. Mr. O'Neill and Anne have asked me to talk to you about the . . ah . . apparition . . you saw at the time of Michel's death.

BLANCHE: So you've heard my story secondhand. But what I really need to know is, Fr. Charles, will any of my evidence help to find the killer.

FR. CHARLES: As ambassador of the Abbess and the Canon, it's my duty to interview witnesses to help them assess if their evidence would be important in any trial.

BLANCHE: Well, Father, I saw a vision of Michel beckoning to me after Michel was dead . .
.

FR. CHARLES: A post-death illusion, no doubt. I mean you just imagined it of course.

BLANCHE: No, it was a real apparition. I saw it beckoning to me the way that you did just now.

She stops suddenly wondering if the priest is the werewolf, puts her hand to her mouth.

FR. CHARLES: *(with especially disarming friendliness)* Yes, my child and did you see anything that might help you identify the werewolf?

Blanche withdraws a pace.

BLANCHE: *(hesitantly)* . . . There was a swirl, like long skirts, then the apparition was beckoning to me the way you were a moment ago with your left hand.

FR. CHARLES: *(urgently, to hold her attention)* So you and the others at the hotel think that the werewolf is a shapeshifter, a disguiser.

Blanche nods, scared and doubtful, she swallows, backs away.

BLANCHE: Yes . . Father.

Suddenly she runs behind a pillar or coffin, followed by Fr. Charles, who re-emerges - by quick change or substitute actor - as the werewolf, still in priestly vestments. The werewolf seizes and begins to kill Blanche who is only partly visible behind a pillar or tomb. Blanche screams. The organ music stops as Elene hears the scream above the sound of the music but by then the werewolf's hands have closed around Blanche's throat and she is silent. Elene listens and shrugs and then resumes playing the organ.

There is a struggle between werewolf and Blanche. Blanche, half-dead tries to run. The werewolf continues to pursue Blanche who screams again horribly just before she falls for the last time, again out of sight. Elene stops playing and gets up from the organ and looks around in fear. She puts her hand to her mouth and peers into the dim corners of the sanctuary.

The werewolf/priest, after seeming to tear his victim and part-devour her, out of sight of audience, runs to the stairs, mounts them, looks around for witnesses and sees Elene. He crouches behind pews and pillars to stalk Elene but she sees him and hides behind a pillar and kneels praying.

ELENE: *(terrified)* Dear God protect me from this monster.

The werewolf hears her voice and rushes towards her, but hears a noise, looks through the church door right and hides. Elene sees the werewolf and screams again, not loudly. The werewolf slinks past her and away and makes his escape from the sanctuary right stage.

Elene continues to be petrified and screams again - not loudly. After a second or two pause **O'Neill enters from right** *holding a gun and approaches Elene.*

O'NEILL: Elene, you screamed? Are you all right? Where's Blanche? A Priest rushed past me just now, head hidden in cowl, was it Fr. Charles?

ELENE: It seemed to be both . . *(shaking and trembling)* . . both Priest and werewolf. Oh, Mr. O'Neill, it was terrible! The werewolf was crawling around here, stalking me horribly just a few moments ago, until I screamed and you came in.

They look around and see no one.

ELENE: It's gone now. I'm so glad it didn't attack you, Mr. O'Neill. *(calling out)* Blanche! Are you there, are you all right!

O'NEILL: I have a theory and a gun. My gun is a large one. My theory is shoot on sight. I suspect that the werewolf is well informed and recognizes me as Enemy # 1. Most likely it saw me coming. It's crafty and skilled but it doesn't like guns . . . It's certainly not here now. *(still concerned and agitated)*

Elene appears speechless with fear.

But where's Blanche? Haven't you seen her leave? I promised to return here to take her home after meeting with the priest. *(O'Neill points to his gun)* I drew this when I heard your screams. You haven't seen Blanche?

ELENE: *(sickly)* No, but I heard screams coming from the crypt just a few moments ago.

O'NEILL: Where's that?

ELENE: *(walking towards center stage)* There - down those steps.

O'NEILL: Of course, that's where we saw the Priest earlier.

They enter the crypt and discover the body of Blanche. Elene draws back in horror and begins to weep. O'Neill puts his arms around her shoulders and sends her back up the steps.

O'Neill looks closely at the body and looks around the crypt. Grimly, he still holds the gun in one hand and moves it about slowly trying to focus on the werewolf.

O'NEILL: *(sadly and bitterly)* So .. I sent you to your death, Blanche. Why didn't I know? Hidden under another persona somewhere is a cunning comedian, a theatrical impersonator, a liar who deceives and destroys his audience. *(addressing the still, mainly unseen body of Blanche)* I'm sorry Blanche, I returned here too late. But I promise you one thing, I'll kill your killer as soon as it clearly stands before me. *(with contempt)* I'll send this shabby actor back to its motheaten wardrobe.

CURTAIN

ACT THREE
The Werewolf Triumphs

Scene Two:
The Priest's Denial

Scene is set in the priest's house Subset Four, and part of the graveyard Subset Three - same as in Act One, Scene One - the Presbytery and Graveyard. Organ music plays in the distance as from the church center and downstage. In the first part of this scene the presbytery is dimly lit and the action takes place in the graveyard central and to the left of the presbytery. **Janice is sitting in the presbytery knitting.**

It is twilight and the tone of the scene is one of regret for the deaths of Matilde and Blanche. There is also a mysterious, sinister, fear-laden element as the question of the werewolf's identity becomes obsessive. A misty pall is hanging over the gravestones, the cypresses, weeping willows and whinbushes scattered among the graves.

Enter left the two guards carrying the body of Blanche on a stretcher. They are accompanied by O'Neill and Dr. Garzon, who is holding Elene by the shoulders to comfort her. *They pause near the side of the presbytery. Elene is sobbing. The well barred front door at downstage opens and Elene's mother Janice - the Priest's housekeeper - comes out, past the barred window which overlooks part of the graveyard.*

JANICE: Elene, what is it?   Who's this? *(referring to the body of Blanche)*

ELENE: Oh, mother, it's Blanche, the kitchenmaid at the Inn. She's been killed by the werewolf in the crypt.

JANICE: No, surely a werewolf can't kill a Christian in a church. Who can be safe?

ELENE: I'm afraid so, Mother. I saw the werewolf. It was dressed like a Priest. It stalked me in the church and ran off only when I screamed and it saw Mr. O'Neill coming with a gun.

Janice shakes her head sobbing.

JANICE: These days, we've seen so much of death. Bring the remains into the presbytery. She can rest there until the burial.

The guards slowly lift the stretcher again. The slow organ music continues.

Enter Fr. Charles from right to graveyard, center. *He's upset and a little distraught, buttoning the collar of his cassock but his manner is calm, friendly and sympathetic.*

FR. CHARLES: Who's this? What's going on?

JANICE: It's Blanche from the tavern. She's .. she's .. the latest victim of the werewolf, Father.

FR. CHARLES: *(calmly and with visible self control, shaking his head)* Surely this werewolf nightmare must end soon?

He kneels and briefly prays in silence over the body of Blanche, stands up solemnly.

FR. CHARLES: *(to the Guards)* Take the body into the parlor.

The guards slowly carry Blanche along the side of the house, past the window into the front door and into the parlor. Elene and her mother watch the removal of the body sadly.

Enter Canon from left. *Twitches, stands to one side.*

O'NEILL: *(to the Priest, as though probing for a reaction)* Blanche was killed in the crypt.

FR. CHARLES: *(upset)* First the presbytery, now the crypt. This murderer has no reverence for either life or sanctity. *(shakes his head)* However, I must go to the church now to hold late night prayers.

O'NEILL: *(delicately)* Fr. Charles I haven't forgotten that your mother was a victim and I'm sure you must be upset but don't you remember that only yesterday morning you agreed to talk to Blanche in church - that was why she was there.

Fr. Charles looks puzzled.

CANON: Yes, Father, you were the one who was supposed to meet Blanche in the crypt, so I hear.

FR. CHARLES: *(stiffening slightly at the sight of Canon Louis, and speaking firmly and slowly)* No, Canon Louis, you are mistaken. I made no such arrangement. I've been praying greatly about these werewolf murders over the past few days and therefore I've been somewhat secluded and made no special arrangements to meet anyone. Of course, I've spoken to a few parishioners as they've visited me and I've conducted prayers in church at the usual times.

CANON: *(to O'Neill)* Surely this isn't what I have heard? Did you not arrange . . .

JANICE: *(interrupting)* Fr. Charles hasn't been away from the presbytery today and very little, only as far as the church, during the past few days.

O'NEILL: *(interested and puzzled, to Janice)* At 11:00 a.m. this morning?

JANICE: Fr. Charles was here in the presbytery at that time. A parishioner called and I introduced the caller to the Reverend just about eleven.

CANON: Are you sure, Janice? Can you swear to it?

JANICE: Absolutely, I swear it.

ELENE: *(defensively of her mother)* Please know that Fr. Charles has been at home all day. I know it. I could hear him praying most of the time. *(as one justifying strange behavior)* It's understandable. Matilde suffered a most terrible death only two days ago and this whole area is terrorized by a killer werewolf. We all need prayer.

O'NEILL: *(with sympathy)* Yes, of course, I agree. This confirms my belief that the werewolf is a masquerador of genius. He had the gall to visit us in the churchyard yesterday morning, posing as Fr. Charles. Then we unwittingly arranged a meeting between the false Priest who was the werewolf and Blanche *(bitterly)* Without knowing it, we handed her into the hands of her destroyer. I admit that I was suspicious of him.

CANON: You were suspicious, but didn't report your suspicions to the authorities? *(twitches)*

GARZON: Ah yes, the authorities *(thoughtfully)* . . like you Canon Louis. That reminds me, you are always close at hand when any werewolf activity takes place.

CANON: *(twitching)* It's my duty to be close to the people. Do you have any proof against me?

GARZON: No I don't but nor do you have proof against me or anyone else. That is my point. We're all suspects.

CANON: Yes indeed, including you yourself, Dr. Garzon. You admit that the werewolf stood among you yesterday morning and you didn't see or at least didn't report anything suspicious. Surely the disguise didn't fool all of you?

JANICE: *(horrified)* So the werewolf stood among us disguised as a priest and we don't even know who or what it is?

O'NEILL: *(with sympathy)* It looks that way Janice but everything is illusion and delusion at this wretched moment.

ELENE: *(puzzled)* Can't anyone recognize him? Surely no disguise could be perfect?

GARZON: Ma'am, I suspect that this shapeshifting is simply magic, plain, old fashioned, deals-with-the-devil, potions, spells and magic. That's why the werewolf is still on the loose.

O'NEILL: *(placing his arm comfortingly around Elene)* Nevertheless, I think Elene has a good point. The werewolf is human. It fled from me earlier because I was armed. Also, why would it show itself to us just to get close to Blanche - to destroy her - unless it feared that she could identify it - perhaps its disguise may have slipped a little when it killed Blanche's boyfriend - Michel.

Elene and Janice are cheered a little by O'Neill's encouragement.

FR. CHARLES: *(slowly)* I just can't believe that this creature had the skill and effrontery to impersonate me.

Janice and Elene look around fearfully and hold hands and O'Neill rubs his chin thoughtfully as he listens to the priest.

O'NEILL: *(comfortingly)* You two dear ladies be sure to lock and bar all doors and windows. Now go inside and rest - the day has been long for all of us - and a sad one.

Elene and her mother Janice slowly and sadly enter through the front door, downstage, into the presbytery, *still dimly lit, and into the parlor/library. They sit by the body of Blanche.*

CANON: *(twitching)* While any one of us standing here now could be the werewolf, yet the main suspect has confessed. As well as Blanche, I have to inform you that in the past few days there have been at least three other killings in the area. Also, it's very suspicious how the suspect Doloree and two other suspects have gone missing again quite suddenly. There may be more than one werewolf you know.

GARZON: *(quickly)* Canon Louis, you surely must realize that anyone would confess to anything in that old abbey with its memories and the museum of the inquisition.

CANON: *(callously)* Perhaps you're right, Dr. Garzon. Who knows? But Pierre, the curator, is no inquisitor and anyway those old machines were banned by our bishops centuries ago.

O'NEILL: By the way, who are the other two missing so-called suspects?

CANON: They are Professor Vermillion and Sergeant Antoine.

O'NEILL: *(shocked, to Dr. Garzon)* Professor Vermillion - of course, we haven't seen her all day and Sergeant Antoine told us himself that he was a suspect.

GARZON: *(interrupting O'Neill quickly)* . . . Yes, Madame Vermillion said she was going to investigate the Abbey grounds for clues.

CANON: *(nodding)* Indeed, she was seen prowling around the Abbey, guarded by the Sergeant, before they both went missing.

O'NEILL: Surely all these confessions and disappearances can't be right when the werewolf is still at large?

CANON: Well, I admit, I'm beginning to doubt that there could be so many werewolves. I'll go now to the Abbey and discuss this with the Abbess and I would value your insights. Perhaps Father Charles will also help.

FR. CHARLES: Certainly, I'll join you in the Abbey in a little while after vespers. I too doubt the wisdom of all these suspicions and even one inquisitional confession. It's all downright primitive in these modern times.

Exit Canon Louis, *nodding, bowing to the others. The faint and sinister organ music continues from the church, floating over the graveyard.*

FR. CHARLES: It's almost time for vespers, so I must go to prepare for evening prayers.

GARZON: Reverend, one thing . . Madame Vermillion is a bona fide forensic scientist and pathologist. Will you help us to find her?

O'NEILL: Yes, Fr. Charles, Professor Vermillion has become somewhat of a colleague to Dr. Garzon and myself. Do please help us find the professor as well as Sergeant Antoine and Sister Doloree.

FR. CHARLES: *(to both)* Certainly, gentlemen. Of course, Mr. O'Neill. I'll meet with you both along with the Abbess and Canon Louis later at the Abbey. *(smiles)* As one of judicious outlook - it's my duty to throw the net wide enough to catch all possible fish, of course.

*He clasps his hands together and bows. **Exit Priest** through presbytery front door and downstage right as though entering the inner church building.*

O'NEILL: Once again, I smell that herbal smell faintly, coming and going. This is a strange and horrible place. Are we also going to go missing? I don't trust these people. I'm glad we came here, Garzon. I wouldn't have missed all this for the world.

They look at each other in some suspicion as they leave.

O'Neill and Garzon leave the stage, left, towards the Abbey as church organ music becomes a little louder. Lights dim, stars flick out. There is silence. After a pause, the werewolf, still dressed as a priest, comes out from behind a tombstone and gloats and howls and eats and laughs and throws bones and earth and stones around. Its claws tear at the graves, their pebbles, soil, grass and flowers thrown widely about.

CURTAIN

ACT THREE
The Werewolf Triumphs

Scene Three:
An Unwelcome Guest Arrives

The lighting now shifts to right stage. Left stage is gloomy, poorly lit. Right stage - the inside of house - is lit dimly but grows brightly as candles are lit. The mood is eerie. Janice is dimly seen lighting candles and Elene playing a slow dirge on an organ. The body of Blanche still lies covered by a sheet on a table.

JANICE: *(her manner homely and wistful but afraid)* This house isn't the same. I've never known it to feel so eerie. It's strange, Elene, but I've been housekeeper here for twenty years since your father died and always when there was a dead body resting there; I always felt somehow that was the end of someone's life, they had died and there was no more to be said.

ELENE: *(playing gently on the organ since her mother began to speak, leaning back and looking to Janice)* Yes, I know, it's like there's a question hanging over her. *(nods to Blanche)* She seems to be saying, it killed Michel and now it's killed me.

Janice nods in agreement, worriedly.
From left and center as from church enters Fr. Charles, *dressed in outdoor, traveling, black clerical vestments.*

FR. CHARLES: Janice, Elene, I have to go to the Abbess now that vespers are over and I may be late in returning. I'm sorry I can't be here with you. Be careful whom you let in.

ELENE: We know there's a monster out there. I saw it in the church.

JANICE: *(pleading)* Oh please, Father, don't leave us tonight. I was just saying *(she looks at*

Blanche) things aren't the same here anymore. We're afraid here on our own.

FR. CHARLES: *(gently)* I understand but that's why I need to see the Canon and the Abbess - it's my duty to try to sort things out with them. I'm afraid that innocent people are being set up as suspects and perhaps even tortured into confessions. I'll be back as soon as I can.

JANICE: Thank you, Father.

ELENE: Please don't leave us alone too long, Reverend.

FR. CHARLES: *(warmly with understanding)* I'll try not to. *(he makes the sign of the cross).* God bless both of you.
(to Janice) Please keep the candles burning in the church for a little while longer. It's still early for those who seek an evening prayer, many are nervous these days - *(Janice nods).*

ELENE: Be careful on the road, Father.

Elene and Janice stand up and make the sign of the cross in a reluctant gesture of goodbye to Father Charles.

Exit Fr. Charles left *through the barred door and towards the castle. Janice bars the door* *behind the priest and buries her head in her hands, distraught and on the point of tears. Elene sadly bows her head over the organ. Elene plays slowly, a sad but strange tune on the organ. She rises slowly from the organ and stares for several seconds at the covered corpse of Blanche.*

JANICE: *(in fear)* I wish I didn't have to go out tonight but *(humbly)* it's my duty as housekeeper to keep the later lights burning.

ELENE: *(agreeing and subdued)* It's a night for bolted doors and windows and it's not right that you should have to go out on a night like this. *(turns round suddenly)* Mother, I'll go *(pleading)* instead. I'm better able to scream or run than you are.

JANICE: *(shaking her head and smiling uneasily)* Don't be silly Elene, I've been doing this candle lighting at night for years and it's second nature to me. I promise to be careful.

She embraces Elene and kisses her, reassuringly.

A hairy-clawed hand appears at the barred door, as of a werewolf kneeling down and trying to find a way into the house. It is unseen by Janice or Elene. Seconds later, the hairy claw appears again and tries the handle of the door and pushes and gropes across the lower part of the barred glass panel on the door. The claw disappears and the door rattles.

As one acting quickly, suddenly in a great hurry, to overrule a change of mind, Janice wraps a light shawl around her head and shoulders and with swift determination leaves through the front door, right downstage, closing door behind her firmly. Her footsteps echo very quickly into distance as . . .

ELENE: *(crying out)* Mother, please, don't leave me.
*Elene runs and bolts the door in fear. Almost at once (false) mother shows her face at door and knocks. Elene sees her through the barred glass and rushes to door and opens it. **False mother enters quickly**, as door is closed, and breathes deeply, holds her heart as one in a state of fear or shock. At this point, it should not be clear to the audience that mother Janice is an impostor but they may well have suspicions. The next episode therefore is subtly ambiguous. Is she? Isn't she?*

JANICE: Oh, my heart! My heart! *(she covers her eyes with her hands)* I can't believe it. I can't believe what I saw . . .

She looks at Elene strangely, with a hint of cunning and a piercing look that says, Do you believe me?

ELENE: Mother what did you see?

JANICE: *(with averted look)* I can't tell you. I'm afraid that I'm going insane.

ELENE: What? Please, mother, you must tell me.

JANICE: I saw someone waiting for me among the tombs.

ELENE: Who?

JANICE: *(shaking her head)* No - it can't be.

ELENE: Mother, I need to know for my own safety.

JANICE: Yes, I know that's true but I must be mistaken. I'm suffering from delusions! *(pauses and points to Blanche's body)* It was her. I saw her . . out there . . waiting by the graves . . Blanche.

ELENE: *(horrified)* If that was her out there then who is this in here, underneath that shroud there?

JANICE: *(apparently terrified)* I don't know. Perhaps it wasn't really Blanche out there. Perhaps it was it.

ELENE: The werewolf?

JANICE: Yes or whatever it is.

ELENE: But how can it just masquerade as almost anyone with such contempt for truth? Who or what is it really? *(doubtfully, wonderingly)* Surely the werewolf can't be Blanche? *(to the corpse)* Blanche, please be at rest. Please don't come back to seek revenge. Don't be restless and don't blame us for not knowing that you were in danger.

Mother looks satisfied, even mildly pleased at this invocation of Blanche by Elene.

JANICE: Yes, Elene, I too pray that Blanche will rest in peace.

They both look at the corpse with both their backs to the door. There is the sound of a finger tapping at the door. The face of (real) Janice appears in the glass outside the barred door - (a substitute, a lookalike, a prop/picture or a video). Outside, the real Janice is amazed that Elene will not open the door and points to (false)

Janice's back and then grimaces questioningly at Elene - Who is that? The inside Janice hides her face from the outside one.

ELENE: *(seeing Janice looking in at window and clutching her mouth in fear, looking from one to another)* Oh mother *(to false mother)* look at that . . . *(to outside)* You're not my mother and I'm not letting you in.

JANICE: *(not turning and keeping her face hidden from the outside Janice, the insider (false Janice) seems terrified)* It's it - the werewolf. Don't let that thing in. Play something spiritual on the organ to drive it off.

Elene sits quickly at the organ and begins to play, badly and with many mistakes, a spiritual but sad melody. Her fingers stumble. The real mother outside continues to gesticulate and grimace and points to false mother inside. False mother keeps her head covered in shawl and turned away from the door, sternly and consistently. Outside the real mother is confused and moves a little way off - no longer being visible at the door. Elene's back is turned as she plays the organ badly and does not see this incident. False mother doubly locks door, driving home an extra bolt. She claws the air and approaches Elene from behind threateningly.

JANICE: *(inside)* It's run away since you started playing. I'll keep a lookout.

Elene looks over her shoulder, Janice stops clawing the air.

ELENE: Yes, mother, please do.

Janice approaches Elene from behind looking at Elene as at a target.

JANICE: I think the werewolf has gone . . keep playing hymns *(she coughs, choking on the words)*
Elene plays louder in panic, then stops suddenly, rises turns, sees Janice threatening, runs across room and faces Janice whose back is to the door. Outside Janice appears again at the window and grimaces and claws viciously at the window, moaning and crying faintly in despair, so as to create some doubt as to which is the true Janice. Outside Janice gesticulates and claws at the window. False Janice hides her face from the door and window by drawing her shawl around her head as in fear. Elene looks at the real (outside) mother in horror.

JANICE: *(inside)* Don't be afraid, the bars are reinforced and it can't break in. Fr. Charles will be back soon and his prayers will drive it off.

The figure at the window continues to grimace and tap desperately at the door and window, again creating doubt as to whom is the true mother. Outside Janice goes off confused and worried. She is seen to re-enter the church, down right stage. Inside Janice acts demurely and quietly when face to face with Elene but has never allowed the outside Janice to see her face. Elene looks, with fear, at Blanche - still hidden under sheet - in fear.

ELENE: I wonder . . ?

JANICE: Why don't we look to make sure that it really is Blanche under that shroud? Just to ease our minds.

ELENE: Yes, there's something here that isn't as it should be. I feel it in the room. A strange smell too. *(she approaches the body)* I must find out.

Suddenly she lifts the sheet and looks - as she turns her back, Janice silently begins to assume a subtly threatening and sinister posture, but changes to a demure and grateful and thankful posture as Elene turns towards her.

ELENE: *(shroud pulled back slightly)* It's her all right. I was worried by a smell of strange spices and herbs in the air and I wondered.

Attention and lights are briefly diverted from (false) Janice to Elene, who relieved and grimly smiling over her shoulder at Janice, replaces the shroud over Blanche under cover of the dim lighting, and as before, with Matilde. Janice silently becomes the werewolf, i.e., her head and arms become that of the werewolf but she still wears Janice's clothes. The werewolf howls and roars and attacks Elene.

As before, in Act One, Scene One, any effective technique may be used, e.g., subtle lighting, a substitute actor moving from behind one of the pillars/large pieces of furniture or even by the same actor removing mask and gloves of Janice behind some such cover. The werewolf throws Elene to the floor, well away from the door. Elene screams as the werewolf attacks; she attempts to fight back, or to run away but to no avail. She stumbles.

ELENE: *(crying in pain)* Mother, where are you? Where have you gone? *(to werewolf)*

Elene is soon overcome by the werewolf behind a couch (or desk or cabinet) so as to conceal the final stages of the murder from the audience. During the final death throes, Elene screams and the werewolf's head and arms can clearly be seen at times. Then both are hidden behind the furniture. The werewolf roars and savages its victim until at last there is a sudden silence as Elene dies. It is clear that she is dead, savaged and semi-devoured.

However, there arises solemnly from the hidden death scene, not the werewolf but Elene, like a specter. The werewolf has taken on her image. False Elene's motions and gestures are a little stiffer than before. Her face is more grim and immobile but she gradually becomes more like the original, without ever being quite as casual, flexible or emotional as before - there is a lingering stiffness in the imitation - an air of awkward hidden purpose.

Werewolf Elene takes the shroud from Blanche and conspicuously throws it over the presumed body of Elene, although this body is still unseen to audience. Elene moves strangely towards the door. She is slightly awkward and ungainly as one trying to find her feet in new shoes. She opens the door.

ELENE: Mother, where are you? Please don't hide. I'm sorry I couldn't let you in earlier.

Elene stands sinisterly at the open door and beckons with her left hand just as the werewolf had done previously when disguised as Michel and later when impersonating Fr. Charles in the church crypt. It's a slow, patient, but somehow compelling gesture.

*Enter **Janice**, frightened, concerned and puzzled.*

JANICE: Are you all right, Elene?

Janice touches Elene on the cheek, questioningly.

ELENE: *(reassuringly)* Yes, I'm fine. *(smiling)* I'm a little upset but come in.

Janice enters. Elene closes door, with an air of satisfaction and bolts it.

JANICE: Why didn't you let me in earlier? I thought that all this trouble had upset your mind. I was so worried about you. Who was that woman you were so engrossed in speaking to? Where did she come from?

ELENE: She came in from the back door *(indicates off stage)* She was just an old woman who wanted to ask my advice and keep her visit in confidence. That's why I couldn't let you in - just at that moment.

Janice looks relieved, but still puzzled, touches the cheek of Elene again, smiles and kisses her warmly. Still smiling, Elene positions herself between Janice and the door, then locks the multi-bolted door again.

JANICE: Good, all is well then *(seeing the body of Blanche uncovered and pointing to the sheet - covered body of the real Elene on the floor)* But what's that . . ? *(she recoils in horror)*

ELENE: *(mechanically)* It's the old lady. She died.

Janice is upset and worried again, and kneels down to uncover and look at the body. She stands up suddenly.

JANICE: *(in confusion)* It's you. It's you, lying dead and mutilated. *(in terror)* I've gone insane. This trouble has destroyed me.

Janice points, in horror, at the body of Elene. Thus, as Janice speaks, the light and attention has diverted from false Elene and towards the body. False Elene turns into the werewolf - as before.

ELENE: *(laughing)* No, you're not insane. You're not mad, dear mother, you're just *(grasping her by the throat)* DEAD.

Janice sinks down onto her knees, stunned and staring and frozen with fear, without any fight or flight. Janice struggles little as the werewolf soon destroys life and throws her dead to the floor - hidden from audience, beside the body of

Elene. Once again there is the sound of tearing, devouring, savaging.

The werewolf - Elene (head and arms a hairy werewolf, but still dressed as Elene) roars and growls, unbolts the front door downstage and rushes out. It laughs and laughs and screams to the sky in victory, howls to the moon and circles the house to appear center stage in the graveyard.

The werewolf creates mayhem in a frenzy of hatred, ripping up bones and rocks - pushing over gravestones as before, but more triumphantly, throwing out its arms in abandon and worship to the moon. It roars and howls again, then stops, jumps and sniffs the air and snarls. Looking around craftily and suspiciously as though suspecting a pursuer, its claws flexed, it rushes off among the tombs and trees still laughing and howling.

__Werewolf__ leaves stage, left.

CURTAIN

ACT FOUR
Trial of a Werewolf

Scene One:
A Jury of Werewolves

Scene is set in the Abbey left stage, subset two if a multiple set is used, as before. There is a long echoing knock on the door. **Enter left the two nuns, Papillion and Prudence. They open the front door to Dr. Garzon and Felix O'Neill who enter from the graveyard.** *They are subdued and afraid, somber. There is a thunderstorm with lightning and rain beating against the windows. The three empty nooses on the wall of the Abbey left are lit up by flashes of lightning.*

PAPILLION: Come in Mr. O'Neill and Dr. Garzon.

Prudence and Papillion bow politely and wring their hands sycophantly.

PRUDENCE: Please be comfortable and sit down. The Abbess is engaged but will be with you in a few minutes.

Dr. Garzon and Felix O'Neill do not sit, but look around uneasily. The Abbey is moderately well lit. If a multiple set is used, the right and center sub-section of stage: the presbytery chamber and the graveyard and church center are all in almost total darkness. **After Garzon and O'Neill are ushered into the room, the sisters retreat and leave left stage.**

O'NEILL: *(sotto voice)* I'm sure we were being followed through the graveyard. Something was stalking us among the tombs on our way to the Abbey. Why didn't it strike us? Does it know that I have a gun? And why is there a sickly smell of strange herbs in the air even here? Can this werewolf be everywhere or everyone?

GARZON: You're right, my dear fellow. Trudging here through the graveyard and the soggy paths I expected something to strike but it didn't. I don't know why, indeed I don't even know what, much less who.

O'NEILL: I agree with you. It's time to point a finger but at whom? We can eliminate only the dead - a werewolf is a living person not a creature of the supernatural.

GARZON: Well, I'm not so sure. I still fear that magic may at least play a part somewhere.

O'NEILL: *(accusingly)* Oh yes . . as with your second self *(scathingly)* - your astral projection - remember?

GARZON: *(astonished)* Who me? Oh no I meant someone else's second self.

O'NEILL: *(slyly)* I mean it was your bright idea.

GARZON: *(flattered)* Oh yes, of course old chap, astral projection, capital idea. And yes, through psychic magic.

O'NEILL: I call it advanced science.

GARZON: Perhaps. But then in that case the werewolf can't be one of the local villagers. The werewolf can pass itself off as educated persons - therefore it must be sophisticated, familiar with polite society, at least by association. Of course, the werewolf must be a master of advanced science, and it just might be cunning enough to conceal its true origins and pretend to be a yokel. *(looks around)* Ugh . . this place is eerie, strangely half-lit and shadowy.

O'NEILL: I can't argue with your logic. The killer could be an educated anyone.

GARZON: But if we're right, that the werewolf is a clever and educated person, this limits the field of suspects to about a dozen.

O'NEILL: Yes, my dear Garzon, like the dream I dreamed last night of a jury of twelve werewolves.

The scene is set in the dimly lit library in the Abbey, left stage as in Act One, Scene One. There are twelve shadowy seats ranged around in a circle. Mr. O'Neill, tired and alone is sleeping, dressed in outdoor clothing on one of the seats. He arises, yawns, sits down, dozes again. Lights fade on left where O'Neill is sleeping as the lights rise on the chairs around him. Eleven of the twelve chairs/seats slowly fill up with the shadowy suspects, entering from left stage.

VOICE OF O'NEILL (ALSO THE NARRATOR): *(strangely, sleepily, as in a trance)* You the jury, whom do you find guilty?
One by one, the eleven suspects stand up and confess, followed by O'Neill, who also takes a seat among them and confesses. The light fades on the others as one by one each confesses. Each of the suspects stand, in turn, accompanied by music clearly representing fantasy or dream with such special lighting effects as flickering colored spotlights or a starry framework of small lights.
All of these effects combined indicate clearly that the appearances are being dreamed in the mind of the sleeping O'Neill and represent a dramatized form of his thoughts about

possible suspects. (If preferred, this entire episode can be videod and screened on a life-sized screen, left stage).

PRIEST: *(standing up, among the jurors)* I truly report I wish . . . I pray . . . that I hadn't done what I did. I couldn't help it. I am Zakotu the werewolf. This is an obscure and poor parish and I was tired of being poor and obscure. In my early days, I was one of the top students in my seminary. If right had been done I would have received a parish in the rich farmland of the north but I had committed a great indiscretion - I hadn't ingratiated myself with bishops and archbishops.

I had always believed in humility and prayer and poverty and dependence on faith rather than churchmen. I believed in all the virtues, but no, the true virtue is crawling to the powerful and wealthy patrons of the church. Lacking this virtue I was sent to this desolate and penniless parish.

O'NEILL (AS NARRATOR): Have you now added sycophancy to your methods?

PRIEST: One night as I brooded bitterly, I had a change of mind. I devoted myself to research and I began to pursue science in a search for long life and power. Already wealthy strangers are coming to my parish to study my secret formulas but they will never prove anything against me, for now I enjoy the protection of the most powerful . . . Yes, it was a small amount of deceit but it brought me ambition renewed.

Priest sits down and Pierre starts to speak.

PIERRE: *(standing)* My body is weak and sick. My brothers and cousins were also weak and sick. They lived and died in poverty and never succeeded in life. Each day I feel troubled in my mind but when I see something suffering it helps me just a little to feel good. I like to remind myself that I am not suffering as much as others - therefore I am superior to anything that is in greater pain. When I see something lying torn and bleeding and helpless, peace enters my heart.

O'NEILL (AS NARRATOR): So you decided that to create victims was the way to improve your own sense of survival?

PIERRE: To see some creature ripped apart is, to my mind, like a cool breath of ocean air to the congested lungs of the swamps. I need to breathe the clear sweet smell of blood in my lungs. Why should I not survive like everyone else? That is why I sought out wizards and learned how to improve my weak and suffering body, into a strong wolfish tormentor. What do I owe to those who are straight and strong? *(laughs)* To torment others is the true fulfillment of the surviving soul for I am Zakotu the werewolf. *(flexes his fingers and then sits down)*

ANNE: *(standing)* People despise me as a low-born peasant but as far as money goes I am the most successful person in the parish. I own the Inn, where travelers take their rest, eat and drink and are entertained, yet I am thought to be just a skivvy. I have long hoped for some recognition, some little friendship or appreciation so I used my money to buy the wisdom that taught me that wealth does not lie in property but in the person. Then I acquired the strength and skills of the werewolf that made me strong in my body and well able to destroy some of those who shunned my friendship. I am Zakotu the werewolf.

O'NEILL (AS NARRATOR): So that those who looked down on you would have greater respect for you?

Anne sits down again and the sergeant starts to speak.

SERGEANT: *(standing)* Mother or Father, I will not cringe or crawl to. I will try to focus the minds of our young people upon their own trades and not to worship the old aristocracy. My killings will never be proven against me because there is no personal hatred from me to them. No one will ever read my mind and prove it in a court of law against me. I am the werewolf but you will never prove it.

People laugh at me. They think I'm a clown. I don't understand this. They tell me to arrest someone - I do it and if this means punishment and death for some, that's not my doing. Jail that man! - I jail him. Yet they've mocked me and laughed at me, so I say: If I'm a clown, then I'm only the clown of law and order. *(staring ahead with contempt)*

O'NEILL (AS NARRATOR): So you have widespread respect. Like the kings fools of old people laugh at you but they greatly respect you.

SERGEANT: I'm not supposed to have any feelings or opinions of my own. I'm tired of being a tool of the rich against the poor. Now I have my own ideas of who to arrest and why and how because I, I am now Zakotu the werewolf.
The sergeant takes his seat and Doloree starts her speech.

DOLOREE: *(standing)* I admit it all – I am Zakotu, the werewolf. It was an evil thing to do, joining the coven of witches but they promised me that if I joined, my superiors would protect me. I learnt that most of the wealthy have achieved their power through witchcraft. They persuaded me to become a witch so that when I killed someone in one place I would have witnesses that I was somewhere else at the time.

O'NEILL (AS NARRATOR): Ah, yes . . . this would enable you to go on killing indefinitely with no hint of suspicion. You would have an alibi for the killing of anyone, anywhere.

DOLOREE: In return for killing the people who were enemies of the coven, I would be rewarded with health and friendship and respect. I am weak now but I'll be strong when they will see me rising up with the full moon on a good night for witches.

She takes her place with the others.

GARZON: *(standing)* No, you're all lying, I am Zakotu, the werewolf. It was my research that one day revealed the method to me in ancient, forbidden, long hidden books. *(bows his head in guilt)* The temptation was too great to feel the blood of youth once again charging through my veins. I thought I'd covered my tracks too well to be discovered. First I mastered the secret art of super-disguise then I visited these parts several times. I was afraid of being discovered when my friend, Felix O'Neill, came here to investigate so I joined him to cover up my dangerous experiments.

(sits down with the others)

O'NEILL (AS NARRATOR): But surely to come here as an investigator with me would place you in an invidious position? Surely this was a dangerous conflict of interest?

ABBESS: *(standing proudly in the witness stand)* Of course I am Zakotu the werewolf not any of the others because I am the descendent of the ancient tribe of Zakotu, who once ruled all of these waterlands and islands before the thefts and ravages of the newcomers. I am a true native of these waterways. I determined to join a traditional order of nuns who have long lived among these peoples and so to extend my power over them as long as possible. So I used the ancient sorcery of the tribe of Zakotu that had come down to me as an inheritance.

O'NEILL (AS NARRATOR): Noblesse oblige. You have a responsibility for the welfare of those around you.

ABBESS: This is my birthright as a true descendent of the Zakotu clan. Yes *(loudly)* I am Zakotu the werewolf. *(the Abbess sits)*

PAPILLION AND PRUDENCE: *(standing up together)*

PAPILLION: All we ever wanted was to discover the truth.

PRUDENCE: Yes, so that evildoers can be punished and prevented.

PAPILLION: People condemn us for working in the old Abbey museum of truth *(with dignity)* We are servants of a very fine lady. *Noblesse oblige.* Her highness, the Mother Superior has a duty to help keep law and order so that her religious and other dependents can live in freedom from burnings and lootings and disruptions of orderly life. Let all things be done decently and in order.

PRUDENCE: If you ask a criminal, did you do wrong, and he says, No, I'm a good man, no definitely not, do you say *(with mock naiveté)* Thank you sir, you may go. Sorry I troubled you. Do you take his word for it? You may say, Look at evidence, but suppose the evidence is hidden - not there - then do you take his word for it? Ah yes . . . is he innocent because he says he is innocent?

O'NEILL (AS NARRATOR): I agree with you. Or do you inquire more deeply into the truth by means of a few tricks and the sight of simple machine aids to memory and honesty? Why, according to some, were those old inquisitors so bad? They looked only for truth.

PAPILLION: Do you let the assassin walk free on his own word or do you inquire more thoroughly? It has been such a grief to us that the greatest malefactors couldn't be put to the test - *(she flexes her fingernails)* - here by our truth machines - they couldn't be arrested because they were powerful or enjoyed the protection of some wealthy one - so they were free to cheat and steal.

PRUDENCE: So my dear Sister and I sought out a wise witch who tutored us in the art of shape-shifting so we could acquire the strength of wolves which we, as weakly women, didn't normally have.

PAPILLION: We have alternated in disguise - each providing an alibi for the other. Witchery learned from the books of the great library showed us the way. We are Zakotu, the werewolf. We are justified because all of those who died were evildoers.

Prudence and Papillion sit down together.

CANON: *(standing up, in some anguish)* I confess, I am Zakotu, the werewolf. I was born with that rare but fatal genetic disorder "lycanthropy" or "wolfism".

O'NEILL (AS NARRATOR): So that you are truly innocent of all your murders.

CANON: All humans are related to primates and, therefore, all humans are related indirectly to all creatures. Occasionally, genetic patterns lose their way, throwbacks we know of, but there are also cross throwbacks - rare occurrences of genetic misplanting - birdmen, horsehumans or centaurs, goat-people like Pan. Wolf-creatures are just mistakes of nature, I couldn't help it.

I was born a half-wolf under the skin *(raises hands)* This is a great advantage to me. I am stronger and faster than the merely normal. Why should I not kill those born to be my inferior. This is the eternal law of evolution. *(screaming)* What right had nature to make me a freak? What do I owe to the world - except revenge? What do I owe to fate except my extra strength and the resentment of an outcast. *(the Canon sits)*

VERMILLION: *(standing and speaking slowly)* You're all wrong. It is I. I am Zakotu, the werewolf. I am the nurse in the night. I am the elusive visitor of Whitechapel. I am the lady with the little black bag. I am the stranger who comes by who people scarcely notice, the casual stranger who fits into the background. None of you guessed because of my acting, but now it's too late for the Abbess and Canon and Priest must find other suspects guilty for some of those weaklings have confessed and to release suspects now would cause a riot - a revolution that would overthrow the local powerlords. My disguise of an impartial co-investigator was the perfect way to find out who knew what and I soon disposed of those who knew or even suspected me.

O'NEILL (AS NARRATOR): Yes, your disguise of an impartial co-investigator was indeed the perfect way to find out who knew what.

VERMILLION: Yes, I am a scholar of the ancient sciences of shapeshifting and have long been among you in one form or another. I am everyman or sometimes everywoman appearing unexpectedly as a companion in the dusk. People go missing and are never seen again. Usually I bury the bodies in the graveyard but sometimes I get careless - perhaps even arrogant and I leave the bodies unburied because it gives me great pleasure to see the same fear and torment on the faces of the living as on the dead.

Madame Vermillion bows and sits. She and the other jurors/suspects remain seated.

O'NEILL: *(taking the witness stand)* I am Zakotu, the werewolf. You may suspect that only I have the knowledge to deceive the masses - ah . . . but think of the great knowledge of the dead.

Can they come back to use their powerful science to tear apart and kill all whom they hate? Only I can explain these things or deceive you and throw you off my trail. These killings have nothing to do with advanced science as I suggested to mislead people.

My true profession is that of necromancer and I have masterminded these killings from afar, from the beginning. The only power I have is, alas, over the dead and it is my mission to make the dead to walk and then to kill the living so as to bring about an equilibrium, an equality. In times past the living destroyed the dead - cremation or burial or mummification they called it - but now the dead seek back their bodies and their resurrected life. Don't destroy them for the dead are my slaves, with them I play like any child with toys.

What pleasure it gives me to send out my toy-things to scare and tear, jump out upon and tantalize their victims. Many and bored are the dead. What joy to give them strength to rise again and go to hide in forests and in houses and jump out upon the living - boo - they say - ha, ha, ha, boo, boo, I am the dead, I have an invitation for you to join me. Come to my region. Here, let me help you join me in the grave, they plead with leaden eyes. And I say, O yes, I am the werewolf or rather the supervisor of the werewolves. The undead all, the zombies wearing the cloak of wolfery to confuse and put together a drama of playacting. What think you of the dead who walk at night?

My toys - joined now by many more. Surely I have a right to be proud of them - they play their childish games of kill so well. The dead cry out in fun - you are my long lost cousin - my next of kill, ha, ha, ha. Run and see if you can loose me but ready or not, here I kill. No longer bored - now laughing are the dead. *(O'Neill laughs lightly)*

O'Neill then becomes calm, thoughtful and contemplative. Lights slowly dim. O'Neill remains standing as dream-like music and a faint, flickering, otherworldly light continues. He speaks the asides as curtain lines directly to the audience, then bows.

O'NEILL:
And now, good audience, you and you
Must pick the werewolf –
Tell me true,
WHO?

CURTAIN

ACT FOUR
Trial of a Werewolf

Scene Two:
Judgment and Mystery

*Scene is set in the Abbey library where **Dr. Garzon and Felix O'Neill** are waiting for the arrival of the Abbess.*

Enter the Abbess *cheerfully.*

ABBESS: I couldn't help overhearing some of that speculation. What a strange work of fiction you two seem to have concocted between you.

GARZON: *(apologetically)* As you noted, Abbess, we were just speculating who might be the murderer.

ABBESS: *(slightly displeased and coldly)* Dr. Garzon, you're not only a very well qualified healtharian, you're a true writer. Yes, some very dubious characters describe themselves as creative artists but you really do have the imagination of a great novelist!

GARZON: *(oblivious of the implied criticism and with great pride)* O thank you, ma'am. You're so kind to . . .

ABBESS: *(interrupting him, turning away and addressing O'Neill sharply)* And you Mr. O'Neill, although no doubt a true scholar of the occult - are not in touch with real people but rather you're somewhere up in the clouds flying among the wizards and witches . . .

O'NEILL: *(cutting in)* So you've been listening to our speculations over a period of time - every word we said . . and for some reason you're upset, annoyed with our efforts *(turning away and putting his hand in his pocket)* After all, we were merely trying to find the werewolf, the shapeshifter.

Dr. Garzon looks at O'Neill and nods attentively. As both their backs are partly turned, the Abbess begins to become wolfish and flexes her hands like claws. O'Neill turns around very suddenly, large revolver in hand, and catches the Abbess unawares in her wolfish posture.

O'NEILL: So it was you, Abbess. You're the werewolf.

He shoots the Abbess full in the chest. The Abbess falls against a bookcase, blood pouring from her chest, mortally wounded. She sinks to her knees. She looks stunned at the blood that is draining through her fingers, unbelieving of what she sees.

ABBESS: *(utterly weak and drained of life and hope)* Mr. O'Neill I would never have harmed you . . if you hadn't come here to interfere with my plans.

O'NEILL: Maybe, but you've lied and killed my friends. Friends do mean something to me . . like Sergeant Antoine and Madame Vermillion - where are they?

ABBESS: They're quite safe, merely being held for questioning with Sister Doloree – inside . . . *(she points to the museum, breathless)*

O'NEILL: *(sadly)* I'm sorry, Abbess but that day you killed Blanche I promised myself that I would kill you, whoever you were, and so I did for you're the werewolf.

GARZON: *(in fear)* My dear O'Neill, are you sure the Abbess is the werewolf?

Enter Canon Louis from right center stage (the graveyard) followed by Pierre and the Sisters Prudence and Papillion from left.

CANON: Abbess, we heard a shot.

Seeing the Abbess shot and O'Neill with gun, Canon Louis, Pierre and the Sisters step back in fear, then, seeing that O'Neill has not threatened them, advance towards O'Neill and Dr. Garzon.

CANON: *(calling out)* Guards, guards, come here! *(to O'Neill)* Hand over your gun, Mr. O'Neill. You can't kill us all. The Abbey is alive with soldiers. Your gun. *(the Canon twitches)*

O'Neill hands over his gun. Pierre, Canon and the Sisters surround O'Neill and Dr. Garzon. Canon - gun drawn, Pierre - sword drawn, Sisters - with fingers pointing shakily at the two suspects. Dr. Garzon and Felix O'Neill are backed against a wall and handcuffed. Canon Louis goes to attend to the Abbess.

CANON: I'll get a doctor, Mother of the Abbey. You're badly hurt. *(looks inquiringly at the Abbess)*

ABBESS: No, I was shot and well shot with a good bullet. Let me die. It was just as I feared. I had a dream so alive and so often that warned me it would be so . . . I would one day be shot but how or when it would happen, I didn't know. So I was wary of guns but to no avail. This was my destiny.

PIERRE: Fiends, so you are murderers come to kill Mother Concordee!

PRUDENCE: *(horrified)* Felix O'Neill, are you the killer or is it your assistant or both of you? How can you kill one so good and kind as the Abbess?

Sisters Papillion and Prudence begin to chatter to themselves in fear, almost half-wittedly.

GARZON: We're not the werewolves. Since when does a werewolf shoot with a gun? If we were werewolves we could break these handcuffs and roar and tear apart all who oppose us. We're just a healer and a detective who seek only the truth - we harm no one.

PAPILLION: Good liars! Isn't that what being a werewolf is all about? But soon we'll have you in our own confessional.

CANON: *(to the Sisters and Pierre)* What you threaten is forbidden madness. No one may torture anyone. Fetch the Priest – he's on his way to the Abbey and bring the guardsmen here. Where are they? Are they sleeping?

Pierre leaves the stage right.

ABBESS: *(dying, sinking low)* No, I wish no rites, no Priest, no ceremonies. My servants Pierre and my two dearest sisters have done no harm to anyone. They only obeyed my orders.

CANON: *(twitches, No, No)* Of course, of course, no blame attaches to them. These *(points to Felix O'Neill and Dr. Garzon)* are the perpetrators of this malice.

Canon Louis and the two religious Sisters recoil in fear and terror of the imminent demise of the Abbess. Canon Louis twitches wildly, No, No, No.

CANON: Surely Mr. O'Neill and Dr. Garzon you're not accusing the Mother Superior of your werewolf crimes?

O'NEILL: Why else is she exonerating her servants, unless she's the werewolf? Why would I shoot her?

CANON: Silence, your words are poison, you scandalous charlatan. I charge you both with murder. Also, you're charged with blasphemy and insurrection, with witchcraft and turning yourselves into sly werewolves.

O'NEILL: I've already told you who the werewolf is. See, even now the Abbess is turning into the werewolf.

Enter Pierre and the Priest with two soldiers. *The guards take over, from the*

Sisters, the task of guarding Dr. Garzon and Felix O'Neill - still handcuffed and standing at the wall - right center. The Priest hurries to the side of the dying Abbess. She has turned into a werewolf in the shadows, unseen to the others. The Priest kneels beside her and then draws back in horror.

FR. CHARLES: *(drawing back and raising his voice)* This isn't the Abbess. This is the werewolf - wearing the clothes of the Abbess. I can't give the rites of final healing to a creature of the pit - this is beyond humanity.

Pierre and the Canon approach the body of the Abbess and lights are brought over to reveal that she is a werewolf. They and the others are horrified at the sight of the dead werewolf which is bleeding and red in the chest where it was shot in the heart.

FR. CHARLES: *(looking around)* Why are these visitors being held as captives?

CANON: *(uncertainly and twitching)* They shot the Abbess and now she's dead. *(places the back of his hand across his mouth in confusion).*

FR. CHARLES: But this is the werewolf! See there for yourself. If this is the Abbess, she has turned into a wolf. It is no crime to kill a killer wolf. Release these outsiders – they've merely been trying to help us.

Canon Louis hesitates, examines the body of the Abbess. He is confused but reluctantly concurs with the priest. He nods solemnly.

CANON: *(twitching, No, No)* Yes, true indeed *(to guards)* Release these prisoners and release any others held in the museum *(he points to left stage and off stage)* They too are clearly victims of the werewolf.

The guards release Dr. Garzon and Felix O'Neill.

The two guards leave *left stage to the presumed museum.*

During this sequence, Pierre and the Nun-Sisters look at first confused and then disgusted. They slink slowly towards the front door of the Abbey towards the graveyard.

PIERRE: You fool, Canon Louis, don't you realize that you and all of us who served Mother Concordee will now be convicted as aiders and abetters. Soon you'll be in jail, then us and we'll all be hanged. Imbecile!

The Sisters hide guiltily behind Pierre.

CANON: *(twitching)* No, I try for justice. I may not be a genius but justice I do try to serve. And you're right about one thing, as close collaborators of the werewolf you three are suspect despite the Mother's last pathetic attempt to get you off the hook. You must have known she was the werewolf. . . Guards! . . . Guards! Where are you, come arrest these?

Pierre draws two knives and throws them at the Priest and the Canon. The Priest is hit only slightly in the arm but Canon Louis is struck in the chest and dies almost instantly.

Pierre and the two old sisters exit *left center to the graveyard. Father Charles kneels briefly beside Canon Louis. The priest shakes his head in sorrow, prays briefly, rises.*

FR. CHARLES: Those killers won't get far. Word travels very fast over these waterways. Soon the whole village and neighborhood will be out looking for them. Even now the local people may be talking about the killing of the Abbess celebrating the death of the unknown one they called, by tradition - Zakotu the werewolf.

There is quietness as Felix O'Neill goes and stands over the body of the werewolf.

Enter the guards with Professor Vermillion, Doloree and Sergeant Antoine.

They look at the Mother Superior stretched out as a wolf in her nun's clothing.

O'NEILL: *(to Madame Vermillion)*   So, Madame, you were arrested and dragged into the depths of this Abbey?

GARZON: *(to Madame Vermillion, stretching out his hands)* Are you all right? Are you unharmed, Madame? Can I get you an escort to the tavern?

VERMILLION: *(trembling in terror and confusion)* No, I'm fine, Dr. Garzon, thank you. Now that I see the werewolf is dead, I feel much better. And . . . So the Abbess Concordee was the werewolf. And you killed her, Dr. Garzon, just as you said you would? Well done!

Garzon points to O'Neill.

GARZON: I'm afraid I can't take credit for that, Madame because it was Mr. O'Neill who killed the werewolf.

O'Neill shakes his head just a little sadly as if to say that killing was no pleasure to him.

VERMILLION: Really, Mr. O'Neill?

O'NEILL: Yes, I realized that someone in authority must have had you all arrested or removed to somewhere for the purpose of keeping everything quiet.

FR. CHARLES: *(to Sergeant and the Guards)* Why are you waiting here? Get out, arrest Pierre and Prudence and Papillion.

SERGEANT: Indeed, we were captured by Pierre and the two guards. I and Madame Vermillion, my charge, were imprisoned alongside Doloree by Pierre and the two mad sisters. It was clear that the abbey was the center of the werewolf's prowlings. So we would never have been allowed to live to tell the tale. Your people rescued us just in time.

Sergeant Antoine and the guards salute and march towards the front door, left stage, in obedience to Fr. Charles's order.

VERMILLION: *(adjusting her glasses and squinting)* Let me join you Sergeant Antoine. You may need a witness to speak to the crowd and testify about the werewolf in order to calm the possible chaos.

SERGEANT: *(to Madame Vermillion)* Sure,

come with us, professor. This will be your chance to give some real help to the people. *(leaving and addressing Fr. Charles)* Thank you for this opportunity, your reverence. Those orders are the sweetest I have ever received. This is my chance to raise up the commonwealth. *(to the guards)* Come, fools, now is your chance to make amends, correct your old mistakes. If you capture these three perhaps I will forgive you for arresting us. I may even reinstate you.

Sergeant leaves left with Vermillion and the guards. *The guards look guilty and confused. Dr. Garzon, O'Neill and Doloree stand together and look down at the werewolf, the Abbess, the dead Mother Superior.*

GARZON: *(putting his arm around Doloree)* You are safe now, dear lady.

DOLOREE: Thank you all for helping me. I am only a poor old woman, a nobody.

O'NEILL: Doloree, you are the survivor of a great injustice, you are only one of many whom we tried to save, because so many people like you have had lives destroyed by the werewolf. *(pointing to the werewolf)*

The lights grow dim and slowly they leave the stage - left through the front door of the Abbey.

First the Priest and Doloree, then Dr. Garzon and lastly Felix O'Neill.

CURTAIN

ACT FOUR
Trial of a Werewolf

Scene Three:
Hopes Renewed

Subsection Five - front stage for the departing scene - representing the street outside the village Inn.

There is now no trace of the sinister and mysterious atmosphere of the previous scenes. There is now no doubt that anyone is whom they appear to be and all speech is frank and without hidden connotations. There is just a hint of sadness for the recent killings and just a touch of nostalgia because of parting friends.

Enter left stage, Dr. Garzon and Felix O'Neill. *They are dressed for travel with cloaks and hats and carry valises. They put down baggage and Dr. Garzon sits while O'Neill paces up and down.*

GARZON: Let's wait here for Madame Vermillion before we join the coach. *(looks at his* *watch)* She'll be here shortly. *(O'Neill nods, but is a little preoccupied)*

O'NEILL: *(nodding again, pensively and continuing to walk up and down)* There's still some turmoil going on here since the two nuns and the curator were captured and found guilty of aiding and abetting the werewolf. There's been a little civil unrest.

GARZON: Unrest, no one will rest until all the guilty have been dealt with - executed, banished, sentenced to life - whatever.

O'NEILL: I suppose it's none of our business now we've done our part.

Enter Madame Vermillion, dressed for travel with valise.

VERMILLION: I'm still not sure how you figured it out Mr. O'Neill.

O'NEILL: A strong smell of garlic and herbs was in her Abbey that night. Now, a werewolf from the outside was unlikely to have invaded the Abbey. It's built like a fortress to protect the nuns. The swish of skirts was there as heard by many victims. Then a stronger clue was the fact that the Abbess read books by early Christian writers who dealt with werewolfism and sorcery.

GARZON: Which writers, my dear O'Neill?

O'NEILL: St. John Chrysostom and St. Augustine, for instance, have written outstandingly on delusion and shapeshifting.

VERMILLION: Hmm . . . I noticed those authors on her table - but I didn't know that they wrote a lot about such things.

O'NEILL: Yes, that was my first clue. And, also, in our final confrontation with the Abbess, I turned suddenly to catch a glimpse of her getting ready to strike us from behind.

GARZON: *(shaking his head)* So you shot her and I admit that I was scared to death when you did that. I've always looked on shapeshifting as sorcery. I hope and pray that the dark powers will never permit her to come back. May she rest in peace. *(sadly)* Indeed, let only those judge her who understand the torment of the soul sinking into darkness.

***Enter Fr. Charles, Doloree, the Sergeant and Anne** from right.*

SERGEANT: *(pointing off stage right)* The coach is here to take you to the steamboat. Ah . . that you should leave so soon. *(takes O'Neill's* *and Dr. Garzon's bags and moves them right stage)* But everyone has come to bid you all farewell.

ANNE: But we invite you back soon - very soon. All the village and fishing people will welcome you. Before you three came - it was a stormy night - now you're leaving on a bright morning. *(she kisses Madame Vermillion on the cheek, and shakes hands with Garzon and Felix O'Neill)*

O'NEILL: Thank you. Again, congratulations on your engagement to Sergeant Antoine *(Sergeant and Anne acknowledge)* now that the Old Abbey is closed and the nuns dispersed and congratulations Doloree on your new job as housekeeper to Fr. Charles.

DOLOREE: I thank you all.

FR. CHARLES: *(to Doloree)* You'll be kept busy. It's a big presbytery but it's better than walking the roads at all hours.

GARZON: *(indicating Anne and the Sergeant)* And some work for you here too, Fr. Charles. I'm surprised that a free-thinker like Sergeant Antoine wants to actually get married.

SERGEANT: *(indicating Anne)* She is so beautiful, I just can't help it. Please forgive me.

(to Anne accusingly) It's all your fault, if only you were ugly I could resist you. To think that the Abbess Concordee killed so many good people and so many wicked wretches like my mother still live. It's an unjust world. It only goes to prove, Father, that there is no such thing as the hand of providence. The hand of providence is of no effect. You must admit it's true, Father.

FR. CHARLES: *(speaking kindly and casually)* You shock us all terribly, Sergeant.

SERGEANT: *(pleased and grinning)* Thank you, Fr. Charles - I do my best. *(to the three travelers, helping to move their bags off stage)* Leave quickly while it's still safe. I think I hear my mother coming.

GARZON: My dear O'Neill, before we leave can you now reveal the name of the person who invited you here.

O'NEILL: Certainly, my dear Garzon.

GARZON: Then who was it, O'Neill?

O'NEILL: I have just told you. Garzon.

GARZON: Who? Garzon? Who is that? Oh, you don't mean me? *(laughing)* Yes, I remember saying that you should look into that werewolf business. And so you did, my dear O'Neill, very well indeed.

The stage remains dim for a few moments then the sound of mob rioting is heard and the window of the old museum chamber (left stage) is lit up where the three empty hangman's nooses have always been seen. The window appears in the light of a red fire, showing the silhouette of Pierre hanging from the middle noose and the two Sisters swinging on either side. Red flames illuminate the shadowy silhouettes. The background noise of mob rioting continues as . . .

O'NEILL: Since you brought about the whole adventure, Garzon, I'll permit you the last word on the werewolf.

GARZON: *(to others)* Thank you, O'Neill. I would only add, here you see Zakotu the werewolf pass into history and peace return to the villages of the great swamplands, but there are some who may disagree, some who will say that elsewhere in the world, when sleet knocks on the window - tap, tap, tap - and when the night is chilly and damp on the spine, when furious raindrops like cold fingers try the handles and press against the rattling quaking doors of the home; when there is a wind insistently whispering - let me in - let me in - then beware of the casual stranger who comes by, for then the Abbess - as a werewolf will live again - beware. That is what some would say and indeed, who can tell?

Felix O'Neill and Dr. Garzon shake hands in a congratulatory mood.

Dr. Garzon, Felix O'Neill and Madame Vermillion *leave the stage apron right. Doloree, the Priest, Antoine the Sergeant and Anne wave at the coach and four, off stage, right. The sound is heard of a team moving off and goodbyes from the three travelers. The Priest, the Sergeant, Anne and Doloree wave towards them - first offstage right, then as the coach, by implication, turns towards the audience, they continue waving, turned towards and facing the audience as they . . . All leave stage right, followed by the sound of the horses and coach.*

Curtain, briefly. Curtain swings back immediately revealing the empty stage. The image of the Abbess Concordee rises up like an apparition in the background - an actual appearance of the Abbess as before lit by flickering lights like a ghost or the image may be presented by backdrop screen, paper or canvas, the projected magnified image of the live actor, on a large video screen, or any other effective imagery. The impression is that of a dominating influence, smiling but sinister and brooding over the entire story in a symbolic way. There is the sound of a furious storm, wind, rain and thunder as flashes of lightning focus again on the images.

CURTAIN

The End

APPENDIX
FIVE FINGER EXERCISE

Simple Instructions on

How to Play the Tunes

Music is presented in the form of tonic sol-fa. Tonic sol-fa is the written form of music for both beginners and virtuosos – those who do not need guidance on timing, arrangements or chords – those who need only the basic tune.

1. Hitting the Right Note
2. White Keys - Stick-On Labels
3. Black Keys - Stick-On Labels
4. Getting the Timing Right
5. Summary

HITTING THE RIGHT NOTE

C is the white note just to the left of the two black notes side by side. Find Middle C on your keyboard. A register is the level of a set of tonic sol-fa. Here is the location of Middle C on a standard three register keyboard. The white note in the exact middle of any keyboard is Middle C (in staff) and Doh (in tonic sol-fa).

Lower
Register
←

← Middle →
Register

Higher
Register
→

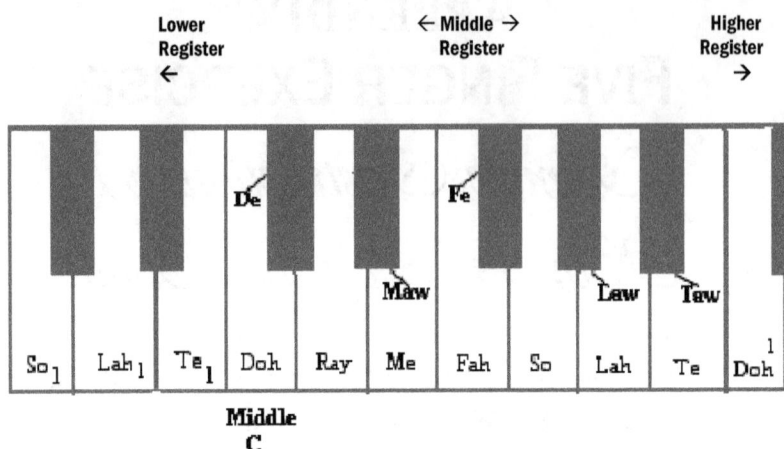

| So$_1$ | Lah$_1$ | Te$_1$ | Doh | Ray | Me | Fah | So | Lah | Te | Doh^1 |

De   Fe

Maw   Law   Taw

**Middle
C**

The tunes in this songbook can all be played on these three middle registers. Larger keyboards may have additional higher or lower registers but these will not be needed for the simple basic tunes in this book.

C is always Doh and going up from Middle C is the central set of tonic sol-fa:

Doh, Ray, Me, Fah, Soh, Lah, Te.

The next note is also a C and is the Doh higher than Central Doh. This starts off the next register of tonic sol-fa notes.

The Middle Set of tonic sol-fa have no subscript or superscript: d, r, m, f, s, l, t.
The Lower Register (set of tonic sol-fa) have subscripts as follows: $d_1, r_1, m_1, f_1, s_1, l_1, t_1$.
The Higher Register (set of tonic sol-fa) have superscripts as follows: $d^1, r^1, m^1, f^1, s^1, l^1, t^1$.

Here is a complete set of labels, for the white and black keys, to stick onto your central basic keyboard.

WHITE KEYS: STICK-ON LABELS FOR YOUR KEYBOARD

LOWER REGISTER	Doh_1	Ray_1	Me_1	Fah_1	Soh_1	Lah_1	Te_1
MIDDLE REGISTER	Doh	Ray	Me	Fah	Soh	Lah	Te
HIGHER REGISTER	Doh^1	Ray^1	Me^1	Fah^1	Soh^1	Lah^1	Te^1

WHITE STICK-ON NOTE INSTRUCTIONS

These are to be stuck on to your keyboard to show you which notes to play as you follow the tonic sol-fa music set out in each song.

1. The seven white notes with subscripts (lower register) lead up to Middle C.
2. Middle C starts off the middle register of seven white notes that have neither subscripts nor superscript.
3. The seven white notes with superscripts (higher register) follows on after the middle register.

Only the last three white notes of the lower register and the first white note of the higher register are shown with the middle register in the keyboard diagram.

THE BLACK KEYS

The black keys in each register are as follows:

de, maw, fe, law, taw.

The five black keys in the lower register
   have subscripts
The five black keys in the middle register
   have no subscripts or superscripts
The five black keys in the higher register
   have superscripts.

Here are the three sets of labels to stick onto the black notes on your keyboard.

LOWER REGISTER	De_1	Maw_1	Fe_1	Law_1	Taw_1
MIDDLE REGISTER	De	Maw	Fe	Law	Taw
HIGHER REGISTER	De^1	Maw^1	Fe^1	Law^1	Taw^1

GETTING THE TIMING RIGHT

(1)   Notes that are grouped together have hyphens between them - to show that they are played together.

(eg: d - f - l). This does not mean that such notes are speeded up, only that they are joined together.

(2)   Notes that are to be held longer than average are written in italics - that is to say they are sloped to the right (eg: *d* or *s*).

(3)   Try to follow the hints at the head of each tune

(eg: slow and simple or fast and warlike).

(4)   Keep a steady and regular beat whether the tune is fast or slow (eg: tap your foot or get a friend to tap out an even measured beat).

SUMMARY

Below is a diagram of all three registers - Lower, Middle and Higher.   Of course, on many keyboards and pianos there are more than these three registers but these keys are all that you will need to play the simple tunes in this songbook

Lower Register   **Middle Register**   **Higher Register**

← Middle C →

← Subscripts →   ← Superscripts →

BRIEF INSTRUCTIONS

1. Cut out the squares and stick them on to the black and white keys.

2. Hit the notes asked for in the tonic sol-fa tunes, trying to hear each melody as a whole and keeping a steady beat.

Key to Tonic Sol-fa Notes
D = doh
R = ray
M = me
F = fah
S = soh
L = lah
T = te

WHITE KEYS: STICK-ON LABELS
FOR YOUR KEYBOARD

LOWER REGISTER	Doh_1	Ray_1	Me_1	Fah_1	Soh_1	Lah_1	Te_1
MIDDLE REGISTER	Doh	Ray	Me	Fah	Soh	Lah	Te
HIGHER REGISTER	Doh^1	Ray^1	Me^1	Fah^1	Soh^1	Lah^1	Te^1

BLACK KEYS: STICK-ON LABELS
FOR YOUR KEYBOARD

LOWER REGISTER	De_1	Maw_1	Fe_1	Law_1	Taw_1
MIDDLE REGISTER	De	Maw	Fe	Law	Taw
HIGHER REGISTER	De^1	Maw^1	Fe^1	Law^1	Taw^1

HOW TO IMPROVE YOUR SINGING

In singing these songs there are seven main aspects of singing to check out and practice towards perfection. (There are also several more subtle, complex and minor aspects which only a real-life music teacher could explain. Each aspect of singing calls for separate exercises as well as putting all six together.

1. Voice Quality
Largely a given, quality can be developed by practice, healthy diet and deep breathing.
2. Diction
Concentrate on sharp clear pronunciation to achieve understanding on the part of the listener. Aim for sounds that most people with standard English, not accents, will understand.
3. Projection
Throw out the voice until all the audience can hear it. Every word must always reach the listener.
4. Phrasing
A phrase is a group of words and notes that are grouped together. Watch how the sounds and words hang together and change the combinations until it sounds right to you in your opinion. What is right for one singer may not be right for another.

5. Feeling

Try to imagine how the sender of the message would feel and think. Develop a dramatic empathy, a oneness with the message of the song so that it comes over as genuine.

6. Rhythm

Keep an even beat or a creative subtly uneven one. Tap your foot on the ground or follow a drummer, or hand claps (see also the section on timing).

7. True Notes

Make sure that the note you play is the right one. Listen to a self-tape and compare your notes with those sung by a friend or played on a keyboard or other instrument. Sometimes it helps to close your eyes and listen well.

8. Find a Teacher

If you can, find a good singing teacher with top credentials or at least get a musical friend to critique you.

THE END

www.ingramcontent.com/pod-product-compliance
Lightning Source LLC
LaVergne TN
LVHW051108080426
835510LV00018B/1965